LOVE WORTH THE WAIT

MY JOURNEY AS A PRISON WIFE

JELISSA SHANTE

Love Worth The Wait ©
Copyright 2020 Jelissa Shante

Copyright notice: All rights reserved under the International and Pan-American Copyright Conventions. No part of this book may be reproduced or transmitted in any form or by any means, electronic or mechanical, including photocopying and recording, or by any information storage and retrieval system, without permission in writing from publisher.

This is a work of fiction. Names, places, characters, and incidents are either the product of the author's imagination or are used fictitiously, and any resemblance to any actual persons, living or dead, organizations, events, or locales is entirely coincidental.

Warning: the unauthorized reproduction or distribution of this copyrighted work is illegal. Criminal copyright infringement, including infringement without monetary gain, is investigated by the FBI and is punishable by up to 5 years in prison and a fine of $250,000.

For more information, email tjpublicationspresents@gmail.com.

…And there's no room for judgment
I want you as yourself
Cuz' I belong with you
And no one else

We have both been broken
Bent into painful shapes
We almost let those old fears
Carry over and get in our way

Every struggle just makes our love get stronger
Than it was yesterday
So here we are now
Ain't it lucky we survived it all
Searching for self in separate rivers
Ending up in the same waterfall

And when we're gray and wiser
The story I will tell
Is that I belonged with you
And no one else
-Amel Larrieux "No One Else"

My dearest husband, thank you for loving me in the purest way possible. I am beyond grateful to experience this thing called life with you. There's no one for me, but you. Forever and always yours ♥

NOTE TO READER

WARNING! With all due respect, before you dive deep into how my husband and I came to be, I need you to have an open mind and an open heart. It took a lot for me to finally sit down and put our story together being that how we can to be is unorthodox. I've battled with how to narrate our story in a way folks would understand, but at this point I said f*ck it (excuse me lord). I decided to be an open book. To be transparent. Our story is unlike any other, yet it is extremely special to me because the man I am doing this thing called life with, means everything to me.

Being honest, at first I was worried about revealing our history. Nervous about folks' reactions to the *truth*. *Our* truth. But I said to hell with everyone and their opinions, they're neither needed nor wanted. It was time I lived my truth, regardless of how unattractive or nontraditional it may be. Often, silence can be misconstrued as weakness, yet it has always been my way of being strong. Telling our story is not about me, but also about the legacy my husband and I are building for our children. He's helped me mature in more ways than I can count.

So this day, I break my silence. I am most grateful for the

man God has placed beside me and I want him to know it. He's been patient, kind, loving and accepting. He's what I never knew I needed.

Going forward, I pray that as a reader, you understand. I've spent most of my life in a shell, doing what others wanted me to do. People pleasing. Going through the motions. Depression. Anxiety. PTSD. Everything. In silence. Until my king came along.

So at this point in my life, I don't seek acceptance from anyone. I just simply ask for understanding as I put myself out there. Allowing myself to be vulnerable. An easy target for backlash and criticism because let's face it, folks gon' talk regardless. Might as well give 'em somethin' to talk about, right? But NO ONE is in a position to judge.

My husband helped me realize that we all have a past and it's up to you to not let it define you and who you are. We all have a chapter of our story we don't read aloud. What matters is that you find someone who'll love you through it.

I found my person. And I am so very grateful for him.

I do want to sincerely thank all of those who have supported us on our journey and continue to give their blessings and well wishes. It truly means a lot.

"Every woman deserves a man who will comfort her soul like no other. Even in the midst of chaos, when the devil tries to knock her off her square, he'll be her calm, bringing her back to character."

PROLOGUE

*E*ver had a moment when the boogeyman was realer than you thought? He'd come and go. Just as you'd start to trust your surroundings, he'd pop up out of nowhere, sometimes he was closer to home than you knew.

I was excited to see him. It'd been a while since I'd seen him. He'd been away for about eight years. My mother had did my hair the night before. I could barely sleep that night.
Today's the day, Jelissa. Two o'clock.
I had worn a blue jean skirt, a canary colored long-sleeved shirt paired with my black Mary Janes. I had to wear the white girly socks with the silk-like ruffles. Hated them. Those damn things always made my ankles itch, but my mother wasn't having it. A child was always supposed to dress like that; a child.
I grabbed my pink purse filled with my mini Polly Pocket sets, so I'd have something to keep me entertained, checked to ensure I had my money, nothing but three one-dollar bills and a gang of coins. I had also had a pack of Winterfresh gum along with the nasty red Peppermint candies my grandma always gave me during Sunday service. I didn't know if it was

my breath or her trying to suppress my appetite, either way, I hated the candy and still do to this day.

I retrieved my green candy apple roll-on lip gloss from my purse and applied some to my dry lips. I never really liked wearing lip gloss because I always wound up licking it all off my lips before the day was over. Plus, I'd been counting down the days 'til this very moment. Pop!

One o'clock.

I was ready early. I couldn't contain my excitement. I grabbed my spring jacket, put it on and went to the front room. I stood in the window waiting. Waiting for the silver Honda Civic.

Two o'clock. A smile crept across my chestnut colored face. I Popped my lips together to make sure they were still glossy and smooth.

Three o'clock.

May be he was stuck in traffic.

"His car isn't out there yet?" My mother questioned.

"No," I replied, my smile slowly fading.

"He said he'd be pulling up soon."

"Okay." My smile returned. He was late, but I missed him so much. Last year before this, I was only seeing him once a week for three hours at a time. My grandmother made the long drive consistently. My whole world would light up at seeing him, just for it to be crushed when he had to walk back through the gray metal door.

Four o'clock.

My knees started to give out on me as I stood at the bay window. My breath fogging up the area in which my face could reach.

Five o'clock.

A silver Honda Civic drove past, turned around and parked across the street from my house. Finally. The car door opened, but it wasn't him. All the life in me had left.

Six o'clock.

"What do you mean you're not coming, Darnell?" I overheard my mother on the phone. "She's been waiting in that window since one o'clock. It's not fair to her. You told her you were coming. I'm not going to allow you to keep doing this to my daughter, having her sitting here looking *crazy waiting on you. Don't make promises you can't keep."* With that she hung up. "He's not coming, Jelissa. I'm sorry."

I dragged my feet as I walked back to my room, leaving the light off. I took everything off and got into my bed. I cried myself to sleep that night. Is there something I did wrong? What was wrong with me? Why wasn't I good enough? Why couldn't he keep his promises to me? I thought. This had been the twelfth time he'd stood me up.

At seven-years-old, that's when I had experienced my first real heartbreak. A father was supposed to be a girl's first hero, her first true love. His job was to show her how she was supposed to be treated by how he treated her. I didn't experience none of that. I had waited eight years for this man to get home, envisioning the bond we'd have, but it was nothing like what I thought it'd be.

My father was in and out of my life, all of my life, yet I still had hope he'd come to fully love me and commit to playing an active role in my life. He was the king of habitual lies and false promises. But the times he did come through, he'd spoil me with clothes, jewelry, shoes, etc. just to disappear for another few weeks to a month at a time.

Six years later, the same man I trusted time and time again, shattered me. My life had been full of hurt and disappointment since age seven. My mother did all she could to protect me, to nurture me, to be the best mother she knew how to be, raising three kids on her own with minimal help. I bet her world come crashing down if she knew the pain her first born had carried for twenty-nine years.

We're always expected to cope with things, but never taught how to heal.

Little did I know, in the years to come, all of the trauma I'd went through would cause me to go looking for love in all the wrong places just to fill the void; the hole in my heart. I wore my heart on my sleeve. Accepting whatever came my way just to feel loved. To feel cared for. A broken girl looking to be good enough for *somebody*.

I just didn't know that Jelissa would never be the same. So, I grabbed my notebook and pen and just wrote.

Love is painful and has brought nothing but sorrow

I've spent countless nights crying no longer looking forward to tomorrow

The lies, the excuses, I've taken everything, even the back seat

Why do I insist on being in a relationship when I still feel incomplete?

The pain stings and my eyes burn

Do lessons come in the form of tears, what if any, shall I learn?

Lord, I'm begging you to open my eyes

Open them; give me the ability to see

That healthy love is obtainable

But first I have to learn to love me

-Jelissa

CHAPTER 1

NO ANGEL

Oh, you see that skin?
It's the same she's been standing in
Since the day she saw him walking away
Now she's left cleaning up the mess he made
So fathers, be good to your daughters
Daughters will love like you do
Girls become lovers who turn into mothers
So mothers be good to your daughters, too

"You just lil' Miss Perfect, aren't chu? You can't ever do no wrong. What; you think you better than everybody, Lil' Miss Perfect? Well, you ain't. And you can't have him. You can't have my father. He's mine! Not yours. You got yo' own father. You get everything. I swear, I hate chu!"

Renee had always been the type of person who created things in her own head. She saw what made sense to her rather than what was actually taking place. No, I never thought I was perfect, nor did I ever think I was better than anyone. True; I had my own father. But his ass was clearly confused on the role he played in my life; thinking he was my man.

He couldn't stand the mere thought of me having another male role model in my life, though. One who I called dad. My stepfather. One who gave me unconditional love and didn't expect anything from me in return, unlike himself.

My *father*, and I use that term loosely, had purchased me my first cell phone to keep tabs on me. Monitoring my calls. You may say, *Jelissa, that's what parents are supposed to do.* Um, no! He did way too much. Disconnecting my phone when he was upset with me. Comparing himself to the boys I crushed on in Jr. High. *"Why you tell them young niggas you love them, but you don't say that to me? They don't love you. You kiss on them, but you don't want to kiss me? I don't understand you, Leesee."* Right; I bet he didn't. He never really tried to understand me. He was too busy expecting shit from me I couldn't give, knowing damn well he barely played an active role in my life.

My sister didn't know the half. Didn't know a damn thing about what her *perfect* sister was going through right under her nose. Bet she had no clue what happened in that bathroom at the sitter's house, for three years. Every Monday through Friday like clockwork. Right around nap time, her *perfect* seven-year-old sister was forced to put her head between some sixteen year's old legs or play with some five-year-old's penis while all the other kids caught z's.

So what, I was an honor roll student. Nothing but A's and B's. I was shocked that I'd still been able to maintain my impressive academic progress while being subjected to the madness. But *perfect*; no. Far from it.

She didn't know that the real reason I grew to love the sounds of jazz music at night was to evade my nightmares. And totally oblivious to the fact that most nights, my pillow soaked up the gut-wrenching sobs that tore through my nine-year-old chest, hoping, damn near praying, I'd die in my sleep. If only Renee knew the overwhelming pressure I was under.

It's easy to say, *"Jelissa, why didn't you speak up? Why didn't you say something?"* Ask the millions of victims of sexual assaults who are now broken adults that same question, then I'll provide you with my answer. I had no safe place. I felt alone.

But once my siblings and I aged out of the sitter's home, well, once I was old enough to babysit myself, I thought my worries were over, until my sperm donor's obvious remarks of hitting on me became more apparent in my teen years.

During my teenage years, I became more rebellious and acted out. My mother caught me up in some mess I had no business doing, which resulted in me being put out of her home and forced to live with my *father*.

He became to comfortable with me being in his home. Walking in on me half naked. Showing me extra love and affection. Referring to me by my childhood nickname, thinking that would soften me. Not knowing, I still carried the burden of his inconsistent presence in my life up into my teens.

During my stay at his home is when he made his first move while we were alone, but soon after many failed attempts and my threat to tell someone, he got the hint. Eventually, I found ways to never be left alone with him and I started to treat him accordingly. Dealt with him on my terms. Using him like he used me.

So no, *sis*, I didn't want your father. I didn't want to overstep my boundaries nor ever make you feel as though you were competing. I just wanted what I always felt like you took for granted.

I'll never have the opportunity to go to a father-daughter dance, but you'll be able to tell all about it. I can count on one hand, matter fact, two fingers, how many graduations or school functions of mine my father has been to, but you'll never know about that. You see, you never had those issues. Your father made his presence know.

The only thing I learned from my *father* was how to lie so

much you start to believe your own bullshit, and how amazingly pleasurable sex could be. I took no joy in the act itself, but the orgasms from the oral he gave me was deniable. Every fiber of my being knew it was wrong, but my body betrayed me. How could I stop? How could I stop him? Who would believe me if I told?

But here I was still broken. Still damaged. Hell, I wanted love. In fact, I needed love. Craved it. Yearned for it. For once, I wanted to experience what you had all these years. You may not have always gotten your way, but one thing you'll never be able to say is that your father wasn't there. While you were sitting there rehearsing the lyrics to Beyonce's, *Daddy* to lip-sing to your father, I was simply praying mine would show up, eventually.

CHAPTER 2

GROWING PAINS

Tears stream down your face
When you lose something, you cannot replace
Tears stream down your face and I
Tears stream down your face
I promise you, I will learn from my mistakes

Life had given me my share of trials and tribulations. As a young teen, I was going through the in-between stages of trying to find myself, figuring out who I was and desiring to fit in until I became a mother at the tender age of nineteen, fresh out of high school.

My pregnancy with my first born was a challenge that I thought I'd never overcome. I hid my pregnancy for as long as I could. The only ones that knew were my best friend, Jeni and the father of my unborn, Raémon, who I'd dated throughout the remainder of high school.

When I finally came forward, the only two options I was presented with were to leave the home or set *that* appointment.

I was pro-life, so I'm sure you could guess what I chose to do. My mother cutting off all forms of communication with me because of my pregnancy felt like a sucker punch to the gut. I remember the conversation vividly. *"I am very disappointed in you, Jelissa. This is not the life I wanted for you. You had many opportunities available to you. I did not send you to Wisconsin with your step-father to be a burden on him. You were sent there to get back focused and do better in school. But I see you are on the same shit out there as you were out here in New Jersey. You will not bring a baby into his house. I already told him that. So, you have a decision to make."*

And that, I did. I went from house to house until I was allowed to reside with Raémon and his family. I refused to go to a homeless shelter. When Raémon's mom had given him the okay, I moved all that I had to my name into the apartment. He'd been living with his mother, father and sister in a one-bedroom apartment. Don't ask how we made it work because we did. Unfortunately, my pregnant ass slept on a palette on the floor. It wasn't the ideal situation for me but I had no other alternatives.

It was strenuous living in a home cramped up with five soon to be six people, but I was grateful to have a roof over me and my unborn child's head. I never grew too comfortable because I did not know when my time there would expire. I was determined not to make this temporary situation permanent especially after that one night that turned into too many.

"All these muhfuckin' people in my got damn house. One bedroom. Tired of this shit. Don't make no damn sense. Lazy as muhfuckas. Den his bitch ass got her laying on the floor pregnant 'n shit."

It is too early for this mess man, I thought to myself. I checked my phone. It was three o'clock in the morning. During my stay, I observed weird behavior from Raémon's mother, Bernette who looked like she could be Angela Bassette's stunt double, shaped like her and all. She had gorgeous chocolate skin and you could tell she took pride in her appearance.

Though her mysterious behavior caught me off guard, to everyone else, it seemed normal. But, it had been the fourth week in a row and I was over it.

She'd woken up at 3 AM, like every other night before, angry as hell for no reason. Cussing, yelling, slamming doors, turning on every light in the apartment, pulling food out of the fridge and cupboards, just throwing it away. Majority of it being food *I* had bought. She was being an absolute tyrant. But best believe when she was up, everyone else in the home had to be, too. This was no way to live. This chaos had caused me so much stress doing my pregnancy.

After countless incidents, I was finally informed that she had suffered from bipolar disorder and had refused to take her meds. The only medication she'd preferred was Mary Jane. And during those times, she behaved like a woman who had gotten some bomb ass dick the previous night. Y'all know the type—waking up at the crack of dawn, playing her 80's R&B, cooking a big breakfast and cleaning the place from top to bottom, all with a big ass kool-aid smile on her chocolate face. The whole house smelling like bacon, eggs and grits along with Febreze.

I did not give into the illusion as I knew Bernette's happiness was only temporary. I was tired of the extreme highs and lows. This was an unstable environment for myself and my child.

There were many nights I went hungry because of Bernette's mood swings, and her just tossing away unopened, new bought food. I had always used my last to feed myself and Raémon's ass.

I had to provide for us when he should've been the one hitting the pavement, making shit happen. The lil' money I was bringing in from Panera Bread—the funky ass $7.25 per, with only twenty-five hours per work week, wasn't cutting it. It was bad enough I was a high risk pregnancy, so I should not have been working period, but I hid that from my job. I needed the funds.

I was busting my ass to make ends me. Raémon was job hunting, so he claimed. It had been four months of the same shit. I didn't know why the nigga thought I was stupid. I had already knew he had had two jobs and quit after the first three paychecks. I had found the checks hidden in his pants, while doing our laundry. I was just waiting on him to tell me about it, but he never did. But bess believe I had confronted him. The more he talked, the more lies he had to put together.

Instead of doing what a real nigga with a baby on the way was supposed to do, the nigga was slanging dick all around town while my stressed out ass had to go into the hospital.

Yes, Jelissa found out everything. There was absolutely nothing that could be hidden from me. I may have been naïve in some ways but I wasn't a dummy. My detective ass had always been game conscious, never putting nothing pass a man.

I was admitted to the hospital the last week in June of 2010. I was due August 23rd but was going into labor prematurely at thirty-two weeks, three centimeters dilated. My baby boy was trying to make his grand entrance and I was extremely worried. I was alone majority of three week stay in the hospital. Raémon made up excuse after excuse to leave me in the hospital alone.

I was broken beyond repair. The same nigga I had given my heart and virginity to was doing me dirty. I'll never forget the message that literally shattered my entire being.

"Alright, Ms. Williams," Dr. Waters, my OB/GYN looked into my eyes with a stern look plastered on his round, Asian face, "though you are going into labor prematurely, we will not stop your body from doing what it naturally wants to do. We're just going to continue with the steroid injections to help develop baby's lungs, so he won't have any trouble breathing if he decides to come early.

Again, we will not stop your labor, nor will we stop your body from contracting. But we will not force your labor either. We will just do our best to prepare and let nature take its course.. We've managed to get you to thirty-four weeks, and your cervix has not changed. You are still three centimeters. We'll release you tomorrow morning. Of course, if you're contractions become more intense, please come back. Sounds good?"

"Yes, Dr. Waters, thank you. Should I be worried about any sort of infection being that I've been walking around three centimeters for a little while?"

"Nothing to worry about. You and baby will be fine. You're not dilated enough to cause concern for any possible infections. Any other questions?"

"No, sir. Thank you."

"No problem, Ms. Williams. You will be placed on bedrest at home and will also have lifting restrictions. I wrote a note for your job as it is not safe for you to return back to work. The nurse will be in with your discharge paperwork, so you are ready to go in the morning. Take care."

"Thank you, Dr. Waters."

Once Dr. Waters left my room, I decided to take tonight to rest up. Though I was relieved that baby and I would be fine, I was in no rush to go back to my living environment. My three week stay at the hospital had been the only for sure way I was getting my three meals per day, giving baby his proper nutrition. Raémon's mother barely kept any food in the home and I was still waiting on my approval notice for the food share program.

It was all bad; pregnant, sleeping on a hard, carpeted floor, and barely able to secure at least one meal every day. The only thing I could remember was the last exchange between my mother and I. Maybe what she'd said was true.

'I believe you're being a selfish individual. You have nothing to offer a baby. You're only thinking about yourself and you're showing ignorance because you know better. Right now, you're on a path of self-destruction....I wish you well. P.S. Once you leave on bad terms, you're not going to be able to contact you're stepfather's family nor this family. If you don't care about your family then fine! You will never hear from any of us ever again. Your sister and brother have been forbidden to have any contact with you. Once they do, they'll suffer the consequences.'

Maybe I should've gone through with the abortion. Having this baby wasn't worth all of the suffering I was going through. I reached over and retrieved my cellphone from the side table. I saw the notification of an unread Facebook message from a chick I didn't know. I opened the app to read the message.

Lencia: *Sooo, did anybody tell you what's going on? I'm assuming not.*

Me: *Excuse me? Who are you? And what are you talking about?*

Lencia: *That answer's my question. I'm pregnant by 'yo' baby daddy, well 'our' baby daddy now, lol. I'm due April 15th.*

Me: *Oh, really? Lol. Is that right? Girl, who are you?*

Lencia: *The mother of your son's sibling. Ain't nobody gotta lie. Where you think he at now while yo' ass in the hospital? With me. Girl, stop being a goofy. We been fucking for a while. We just fucked today in my unty bathroom. I'm here to stay so you better get used to it.*

Me: *Whatever. You done?*

Lencia: *Bitch, Yousa a goofy. Where you think he be at when he don't come home 'til three in the morning? You gon' see. Your son will be having a sister or a brother soon, so . . .*

I left her on read and damn near dropped the phone. How did she know what the sex of my baby was? How did she even know I was in the hospital? Something in me knew she was telling the truth, but I couldn't wrap my head around it. The truth was the hardest pill to swallow. I did my research once I left the hospital, only to discover that the broad was indeed pregnant.

When I confronted Raémon that night he came back to the hospital, he denied being the father, but not once did he mention not sleeping with her. To add insult to injury, I found out that the girl lived around the corner from his mom's house.

As the truth continued to reveal itself, all I could do was cry. 'Why didn't I get the abortion? I should have listened to my mother.'

My baby boy, Rae'Jon was born July 29th, 2010, about a month early. Thankfully, he was healthy. That's all that mattered to me. It was unfortunate that we had to go back to a one-bedroom apartment.

The first four months, I suffered severely from postpartum depression. I could not eat nor sleep. Rae'Jon had developed colic. I wasn't producing enough milk nor making any money to purchase formula. I was in a horrible position. A single mother with a deadbeat ass nigga for a father who was barely present. *Maybe adoption should have been explored.* I was tired. I had moves to make.

Rae'Jon had been my purpose. I had someone besides myself to live for. It was time for me to get my life together. Not only for the sake of myself but for the child that now depended on me. I was determined to prove to not only my mother but myself that *I* could be a damn good mother.

By February of 2012, I had gotten my first one-bedroom apartment. It wasn't much but to me, it was everything. It had been a long time coming. I was tired of house hopping. My son deserved a stable and safe environment and providing him with that was my top priority.

I took up a job in the healthcare field as an in-home caretaker, providing one-on-one care to the elderly and disabled. I had grew accustomed to this type of work when I started caring for my uncle at the tender age of sixteen. He had been diagnosed with Autism and Cerebral Palsy. Caregiving came with so much ease and the scheduling was flexible, so I opted to stay within that line of work.

I worked my ass off though. I barely saw my son who had been two-years-old at the time. Every day like clockwork, I completed my first shift, went home to nap for an hour then went back to my second shit. It was what I had to do to bring home the money seeing as his sperm donor had been M.I.A majority of the time. His ass only came around when he needed something—food, money or a place to lay his head.

It broke my heart every time I saw my child cry whenever I had to leave him. I knew I had to make some much needed changes being that my presence in his life started to become nonexistent, and I became damn near a stranger to my own child. And that just didn't sit right with me.

Though it fell on my shoulders to provide my child's every need, the most important need of his I was ultimately neglecting was his need for quality time and attention. I was all my baby had.

CHAPTER 3

LOVE IN THE WRONG PLACES

Doing what you're doing
Just to get to where you're going
Yeah, I see you baby
Just don't lose yourself along the way...

June 2012

I was on my way to work. I was ready for the day to be over with as I had had a full schedule and wouldn't be seeing my baby boy until later on that night.

I boarded this bus and took my seat towards the left by the window per usual. I took pleasure in sitting alone closest to the window. I used that hour bus ride to clear my head and envision where I would be in my life within the next five years or so.

I was minding my own business when I noticed an older

gentleman fumbling with a cellphone, lips moving. I looked out the window then looked back.

His lips were still moving as he continued to look in my direction, yet I could not hear anything. I absolutely hated being spoken to in public places. I was the type of person who always walked around with my head down to show those around me that I was not up for nor open to any type of conversation. I just wanted to be left alone and get to where I was going in peace.

I looked away and continued bopping my head to the music. I glanced up and noticed that this same gentleman was now making direct eye contact with me, *still* moving his damn lips. I released the attitude that built up within me, pulled my headphones out of my ears and looked in his direction.

"Hey, Queen. I don't mean to bother you. I see you're not really in the mood, but if you can help me, I'd gladly appreciate it. I can't seem to work this phone."

"Okay. What are you needing help with?" I managed to give a slight smile to lighten up my resting bitch face.

"I am trying to get to this address here," he replied, showing me the address on a piece of paper. "Can you tell me where this bus goes and how I can get to this location? What bus do I need to get on next?"

I went ahead and explained how he could utilize the map app on his mobile device to see different bus numbers, bus stop locations, schedules and how to connect from one bus route to the next.

"Thank you so much, Queen! I knew you could help me figure this out. I definitely need you in my life. We most definitely do."

We. Whose we?

He waved toward the back of the bus. I didn't care enough to look back until I heard the bass from another gentleman's voice. "Is it okay if I sit here?"

I looked up to see who the voice belonged to and was met with a smile and dimples. "Sure."

"Thank you for helping my father. If it had been left up to him, we would have gotten lost and never made it to our destination."

"I told her we needed her in our lives, son."

"Most definitely, Pops. And she gorgeous. Looking like she on her way to work. Are you? Or are you just getting off? If I am being too nosy just let me know." He smiled again, showing off his silver caps on his front two teeth. His shoulder-length dreads were neatly styled to accentuate his smooth, chocolate skin.

"Um, I am on my way to work actually."

"Okay, Well, my name is Ahmad. My Pops; Armani."

"Hello."

Ahmad chuckled. "So, we can't get your name?"

"I guess. Jelissa."

"That's a pretty name."

"Thanks."

"I've never seen you on this bus before. You live around here?"

"Now, you're asking to many questions."

"My bad, Queen."

"Be careful, son." Armani spoke up. "Beautiful looks like she don't play."

I gave Ahmad that, *and I don't* look.

"Can we be friends? Is that alright with you?"

"I guess." I replied, giving him a small smile. It had been too much word play for me and I was ready to move towards the back of the bus until my stop came.

"Wait, how old are you?" He grinned. "I don't want to be getting into no trouble."

"Old enough."

"Lemme see some I.D. You look like a little girl, no disrespect."

I stared at him for a split second then proceeded to pull out my I.D.

"Ohhh, okay. My bad. You just look so young. You're very gorgeous though."

"I hear that a lot. Trust me. Um, you gon' show me some I.D. You look older." I became less tense as my stop was approaching. I started gathering my things.

He showed me his I.D. and he'd definitely been older. By ten years. "When can I see you again?" He asked with all seriousness in his eyes.

"If you are on this bus the next time I am."

"Damn, that's cold-blooded."

I chuckled.

"Ladies and gentlemen, a smile. We got her to laugh a lil'. Well, it was nice meeting you, Jelissa."

"You too, Ahmad."

"Yes, thank you so for your help," Armani said, grinning from ear to ear.

"Hopefully, I'll see you again?" Ahmad asked, quizzically.

"I don't know. Maybe. Maybe not."

"Just cold-blooded."

He smiled once last time as I made my exit towards the back of the bus. And like that, I had completely forgotten about this odd exchange until he showed up again.

The next few weeks, I had kept running into Ahmad and his father, Armani. I didn't think it was by coincidence either. He had always been on the same bus around the same time and day I had been. I was beginning to think that the man had been stalking me.

Every time he saw me, he made it his thing to sit either next to me or across from me, making small talk. He was persistent in getting to know me, so I finally relented and we exchanged numbers. I just didn't know exactly what I was getting myself into.

"*Hello, is this Jelissa?*" The first time I heard T.J.'s voice, it was something about the deepness in his tone that spoke to my soul. I didn't know what it was about him, but I was immediately drawn to him.

"*Yes, this is she.*" *I replied nervously.*

I could not believe I was finally able to put a voice to the name. Ahmad had spoken highly of his 'favorite brother', T.J. I can't lie and say I never ear hustled on many conversations spoken within the family about the infamous T.J. I was nosy. I had to know who this T.J. person was. He had been paying so many of his family member's bills and sending them money. From what I gathered, they were dependent upon him, especially his elderly grandmother, Wendella.

It was crazy how small this world was. Wendella had been one of my clients. She was sixty-two-years-old with vibrant Hershey colored skin, always rocking her gray cornrows to the back. She was a Pisces like me, birthday a day before mine. She was a straight forward woman that was great at cooking, and always kept things real. I respected her so much and had grew to love her.

I provided care for her three times a week. She was one of my all-time favorite clients, so I always jumped at the opportunity to pick up extra hours with her. Not to mention, I needed the extra money and she had allowed me to bring my child with me when I couldn't secure child care.

Rae'Jon had taken to her rather quickly, and she in turn, spoiled him rotten. When it came to family visiting her, Ahmad had coincidently always came around on the days I was assigned to work with her, other than that she was alone majority of the time.

She loved her some T.J. though. That's all she'd ever spoken about when we were alone. He was her favorite grandson because of how often he checked on her and provided for her.

She would always say to me, "*Out of all my grandkids, I can tell T.J. loves me the most. Ahmad don't ever check on me like he should and he out here. He just recently started coming around when he met you. Other than that, them damn kids don't really about me. But wait until you meet my grandson, T.J. You gon' love 'em.*"

After hearing all of that, I couldn't wait to meet him either. I couldn't fathom how an incarcerated man could do so much for his family from the inside, while the free men in his family couldn't find two pennies to rub together. That alone piqued my interest.

"Damn, are you black?" T.J. asked, sounding like he'd been caught off guard.

"Yes, I'm black, why would you ask me something like that?" *Hell, what if I wasn't. Then what.*

"Because you sound proper as hell." He laughed. His laugh was so sexy to me. I immediately felt guilty while Ahmad stood a few feet away from me texting away on his other phone. I grew irritated and rolled my eyes at him.

"Um, yes, I'm black. I just talk a little bit proper because of where I grew up school. What, you never been around any women who talk *proper*?"

"Not in Chicago. The sistahs out there be more hood than the niggas be. But anyway, I don't care about all of that. I'm just glad that you are. It's about time one of my brothers embrace that black beauty. All dem niggas be tryna fuck on is red bones, white girls, and Spanish women."

"What about you?" I don't know why I asked him that but curiosity got the best of me.

"I love black women. There ain't another race on this Earth that is more beautiful than my sistahs. That's how I feel." He paused for a minute as the prison's phone recording came on. "All calls other than properly placed attorney's calls may be monitored and recorded."

"But anyway," he continued, "how is he treating you? How is everything going?"

I glanced over to Ahmad from the corners of my eye. I could tell he was trying his best to fake ear-hustle T.J. and I's conversation. I knew he was ready to get his phone back from me.

When we made eye contact, he smiled and began to walk down the hallway. I sighed. Something in me didn't feel right, but our business was our business. I wanted so bad to tell T.J. how I had found naked pictures and messages from some chick named Deidra in dude's phone but I lied instead. "It's okay."

"Nah sis, don't be lying to me. I already know how bro 'nem be finding it acceptable to crap on the sistahs when they knock one. I can tell in your voice that you are going through some shit, huh?"

My stomach did somersaults. How did he know? I wanted to confirm what he thought he knew so bad, but I didn't know if this was a trap by Ahmad, and T.J. would probably run right back to him and tell him whatever I really wanted to say to him, so I held my tongue. "Every relationship has their ups and downs, ours is no different." I responded flatly.

"Yeah, awright. Look sis, I watched my father drag my mother through the mud. He beat her down in every way that you can think of, and she took blow after blow until she passed away at the young age of thirty-four. I don't give a fuck how you feel about my brother, or any other nigga for that matter, you never allow for no man to break you. Allah placed your womanly intuition inside of you for a reason. If somethin" don't feel right, it probably ain't. Protect yourself, do you understand me?"

I felt breathless. I began to nod my head as if he could see me. It wasn't until he kept repeating the words hello that I snapped out of my zone. "Yes, I understand you. I hear you."

He laughed that sexy laugh again. "Good, now what's up with some flicks so I can see how you look?"

That really caught me off guard. "Um, pictures? Why you wanna see how I look?"

"Yes, and I don't know, I just do. I got a feeling you and I are going to be real close. Besides, if you're going to be a part of this family then I definitely gotta protect you just like a li'l sister. You and my new nephew. I already told you how the fam like to crap on the black Goddesses that be passing through. That shit is foul. That ain't finna happen to you. I got this, even from here." He stated, confidently.

I smiled. "Aw, that sounds nice. I got you too, then. The only pictures I have right now are of me and my two-year-old son, Rae'Jon. Is that okay?"

"Yeah, that's cool. Are you gon' send them for real though?"

"Yes, I will."

"Ohhhkayy now. People have a habit of telling me they gon' do somethin' for me and they never follow through. I don't want us to get off to a bad start. You sure you' gon send those pics?"

"Yes, I am sure. I will get them to you. I promise." I looked up and saw Ahmad heading in my direction, at the same time the phone telling myself and T.J. that we had only one minute left to talk.

Ahmad stopped and stood over me. "You still talking to him?"

I plugged my right ear and frowned at him. "It just said there is only one minute left to talk."

"Okay sis, make sure you send me those pics. Get my information from Ahmad. Keep yo' head up and be strong. You are a Queen. Please don't forget those pictures."

"I won't. Thank you and you be safe in there."

I handed the phone back to Ahmad and went back

towards the living room to go take a seat next to Rae'Jon. Ahmad followed behind me.

"What did he say?" Ahmad asked.

"He didn't say too much of anything. Just wanted to know who I was and told me to send him pictures of Rae'Jon and I."

"Yea, I'd been telling him for the longest that I'd send pictures of y'all. I been forgetting. Just been super busy. I don't want him to feel like I forgot about him, so make sure you send him those pics. Write him too. Just let him know how we all doing. That's my baby brother and I love him."

Yo' ass always claim to be busy. "He also said he was happy that I was black. He mentioned that his brothers usually go for lighter women."

Ahmad chuckled. "Yeah, my pops don't play. He like us to make sure our women are gorgeous. I usually bring home women of different races. You are one of few black women I've actually been with. I told him you was Jamaican, too."

I don't know why he'd told that lie. That goes to show how much he *hadn't* been listening to me. Never told him I was Jamaican. I told him that was sister and her family was. I was so offended by that last stupid ass comment he'd made. It was time for me to go and I knew the next bus would be coming soon. "Well, I'm about to leave. I'm getting a migraine." I walked over to his grandmother.

"Alright Ms. Wendella, I am about to head out if you don't need anything else."

She reached out to hug me. "Baby, thank you for doing a good job with everything. I love you, and I will see you tomorrow I'ma need you to go grocery shopping for me."

"Sounds good. I'll see you tomorrow."

"See you tomorrow, baby."

I put Rae'Jon's coat on, gathered his things and walked right past Ahmad. I had had enough of him and his arrogant ass attitude.

CHAPTER 4

WHAT LOVE IS AND WHAT LOVE AIN'T

Hennessy plenty weed, do you have anything stronger
I don't care give it here
Wanna make this high last longer
Unafraid unaware can't you see I am dying
Wanna feel what is real anything is worth me trying

I was about four months into my relationship with Ahmad when things went from sugar to shit. He was always leaving me at his home, constantly lying and always coming home at damn near 3AM from his *meetings*. I knew better. The nigga had me mentally drained. I knew something wasn't right. I just couldn't shake this feeling.

The mental stress of the relationship and me working like a dog started to take its toll on me. I rarely ate, barely exercised, and hardly slept. Slowly but surely my body began to get weaker and weaker to the point that I grew faint and passed out a lot.

I couldn't understand what was really wrong with me. All I knew was that I was searching for unconditional love inside of a man who only cared about himself. While I grew to know the type of individual I was dealing with, I couldn't bring myself to break away from him.

My entire life I had been led to believe that I, as a woman, was never good enough. That I wasn't attractive enough. I was too skinny, had big lips and geeky. And if I did just so happen to attract a man, he never stay for long. So as you could've imagined, my self-esteem and self-worth was extremely low. I had spent majority of my life trying to fit into a box that was never shaped for me.

My father had never taken the time to help with my self-esteem growing up. He was in many ways a mirrored reflection of Ahmad. He was selfish and him-focused. I had never had any prominent male role models in my life. Man, I was so damn tired of these rollercoaster rides with men. I was just so ready to get off.

Even though I was finding it hard to release Ahmad because of my own insecurities, there was a straw that had finally broken the Camel's back.

It was a cold November night, snow fell in thick patches from the sky, and the wind was blowing so harshly that my face felt frozen as the Metro city bus pulled up to its stop, allowing for me to get on it.

It was mildly packed with people and smelled of cigarettes and alcohol. The unpleasant scent caused my head to hurt even more. The intense migraine might have originally come from the fact that it had nearly been thirty-six hours since I had eaten a decent meal that didn't involve crackers, or a boiled egg. My appetite had been nonexistent.

Ahmad was getting the best of me, and my stupid ass was struggling to find the strength to let him go so that I could find myself again. Not only was I neglecting myself because of the turmoil that he was taking me through but I was neglecting my two-year-old son, Rae'Jon just as bad.

It had gotten to the point where I just didn't have the strength, nor drive to deal with the duties that it took to be a mother to a toddler child. My every thought was surrounded around a man that was literally killing me without the use of a weapon.

Minute by minute, hour by hour, I detested myself for how I neglected to be emotionally present for my child during this relationship with Ahmad. I had to break free, and in order for that to happen it was imperative that I found the woman of strength that I knew lived deep inside of me.

When I stepped off of the city bus the snow really started to come down. I damn near passed out. I was determined to get to my destination.

The wind was blowing so hard that I felt like it was trying to push me over. I was down to about ninety-five pounds, and as weak as I had have ever been. I fought against Mother Nature's elements until I made it to Emergency Room entrance.

I approached the help desk barely able to stand straight.

"Hi there, how may I help you?" The red-headed nurse asked me.

"Yes ma'am, I need to be seen."

"What's going on? What are your symptoms?"

"Light-headedness, my skin feels warm to the touch, I feel nauseous, I can't keep anything down, and I have been passing out a lot." I ran down the list of things I'd been experiencing over the last month.

"Any vomiting?" She asked, not looking up from her computer.

"No ma'am."

"Okay, can I get your name and date of birth?"

"Jelissa Williams. Three-ten-ninety-one."

"Sounds good. Well, I've got you all checked in. Just have a seat right over there and the nurse'll be right with you to bring you back."

"Thank you." I took a seat to the far left of the small waiting room. I don't know why it'd taken me so long to make this trip. My body had had enough. I couldn't carry on like this any longer.

Once I was called to the back, I went through the routine questionnaire that I'm sure they asked all patients. I had been getting my period so I wasn't concerned about pregnancy, but that didn't stop them from requesting a urine sample, testing my blood, and running a CT scan.

I had waited for over two hours before my results from all the testings came back, and during that time they had hooked me up to an I.V. where I'd received two bags of fluid. As my last bag was finishing up, a tall and lanky gentlemen who looked like Bill Nye, the science guy.

"Alright, Ms. Williams, I'm Dr. Winston. I have your test results here. Let's start with your health overall. You were extremely dehydrated which is why you were given the two bags of fluid of course, so I am sure you probably have to go to the bathroom." He offered a light chuckle as he continued, "you are definitely going to need to eat more as your iron and calcium levels are extremely low. Do you feel cold all the time?"

"Yes sir, I do. I am always cold."

"Welp, your low iron levels would surely be the reason for that, so along with eating better, we're going to give you some iron supplements as well as Zofran for nausea to help you keep an appetite. Also, your blood test. It came back positive for pregnancy. We couldn't detect pregnancy within your urine because you are in the early stages, about three weeks-,"

"Pregnant? How can that be? I had my period." I was in complete disbelief. Although Ahmad and I hadn't been practicing safe sex, I didn't think anything of it being that I got my period regularly.

"That is not uncommon, Ms. Williams but yes ma'am, you are definitely pregnant. You will need to schedule a follow-up with your regular healthcare physician for an ultrasound and such. If you don't have any other questions, comments or concerns, I'd like to have the nurse bring in your discharge paperwork. Seems like you are 'bout ready to get out of here."

"Absolutely. I am okay. I will make an appointment next week. Thank you, Dr. Winston." When the doctor walked out, I immediately picked up the phone to call Ahmad. He picked up on the first ring.

"Hello?"

"Hey." I replied, dryly.

"Oh hey, baby. What's goin'?"

"I'm pregnant. That's what's goin' on."

"Pregnant? Really? But you were still gettin' your periods. How can that be?"

I was growing aggravated by the second. "Uhm, pregnancy is a result of unprotected sex and we had a lot of it."

"Yea, we sure did." He laughed. "Well, this is great news. I wasn't playing about making you my child's mother."

"I don't want this baby."

"Wait, what? Don't say that. Come by tomorrow so we can talk."
"There's nothing to talk about. I don't want this, baby."
"Where are you so I can come pick you up?"
"Almost home," I lied. I hadn't even received the discharge paperwork from the ER. I just didn't want to be bothered with dude and his bullshit. A switch in me had flipped once the doctor told me I was pregnant.
"Okay. Can you come by the house tomorrow?"
"I'll letchu know, Ahmad." I disconnected the call before he had the chance to respond.

When I had finally got my discharge paperwork, I gathered my belongings and headed to the waiting room. From there, I could see the bus stop. Though I didn't want to catch the bus late at night, I refused to deal with Ahmad. But God must've been on my side because the same nurse that I'd seen at check-in earlier had offered me a cab voucher.

I called the cab service and ordered me a cab. I was so relieved when I finally arrived home. I had had a long night. Pregnant? Really? Me? Pregnant? Couldn't be. But then again, of course. It was bound to happen.

I decided to take some much needed time to myself. Ahmad blew my phone up repeatedly, every single day via text messages and calls begging me to come over and talk to him. But to me, it was pointless because I had already made up my mind about this pregnancy. I'm not gon' lie and say I didn't know what I was getting myself into when I made the decision to stop taking birth control and sleep with him unprotected. I knew what I was doing. I was aware.

I am woman enough to admit that I knew the consequences of my actions, but as time went on, I had saw a totally different man and no longer welcomed the idea of a baby. I was done.

CHAPTER 5

OVER IT

If you cannot stay down
Then you do not have to pretend
Like there is no way out
I shoulda never let you in
'Cause you got me face down

A woman never knows how strong she is until she's placed in a position to be just that. Strong. I was so ready, appointment and all to go through with the procedure but I didn't. My best friend, Jennifer gave me the courage and the reasoning I needed cancel the abortion and keep my child. A'Jhani wouldn't be here to this day if it wasn't for God communicating to me through my friend.

The first three months were the hardest for me especially after Ahmad found out that I was pregnant. He gave me every bit of game he had inside of himself. He told me that it was meant for us to have this baby. He said that God had already made up his mind that he and I were supposed to be together.

He even told me that he loved me and promised to never hurt or cheat on me again.

He threw so much game at me in such a short amount of time that I almost believed him. I found myself slowly easing back into his web of deception and manipulation, and right before I became incarcerated under his spell Jennifer would pull me back from under him, and only then was I able to shut off those ignorant emotions that most young twenty somethin' year old's got. It seemed like the more I distanced myself from him, the harder he tried to get me back. But it didn't matter, there was nothing moving. I blocked his ass and endured the remainder of my pregnancy alone. I didn't need nor want him around. The last month of my pregnancy, he popped up at my house, just asking to be present at the birth. I gave him that opportunity.

A'Jhani was born healthy and strong on July 29th 2013, sharing a birthday with his older brother, Rae'Jon who was turning three at the time. Imagine being three and spending your birthday in the hospital.

I was thankful to have to happy and healthy boys despite the difficulties of both pregnancies. Instead of me being able to relish in the fact that God had given me a healthy child, Ahmad attacked me about the naming of our son.

He wanted our son to have this super Muslim or Arabic name, and I wasn't going for it. Ahmad had already changed his last name to reflect that of his Islamic faith, and he said that it was important that his son had the same blessed and ordained name.

I told him I was a Christian, and we would split the naming of our child. He fought me tooth and nail, even managed to call me out of my name a few times before I allowed him to give A'Jhani his middle name. I gave my son his first, and last name. I had stood my ground against him and I felt damn proud of myself for doing so.

⁓

*C*o-parenting with Ahmad proved to be an issue with him right away. Prior to A'Jhani being born, Ahmad and I had very little contact. There was no need for it, and I stood on that. Now that A'Jhani was in the picture, Ahmad thought that our son gave him some rights to me. He started to slowly ease his way back into my life until he was prominently grounded.

Ten months after A'Jhani was born, my funds stsrted getting very low, and the bills were piling up. While I still worked for Wendella every now and then, but because Ahmad was always over her place I passed up on a lot of work hours that I could have had working for her.

In the spirit of working toward my independence from him, I decided to pick up other elderly clients to bring in some income. I also had to take on a second job. Financially strapped and not yet ready to trust a daycare to look after my son, I decided to work things out with Ahmad so that he would keep A'Jhani while I worked. It felt like the safest bet at that time.

His stupid ass had arrived to my apartment nearly forty-five minutes late. I was fuming. I hoping to arrive at the job fifteen minutes early but his tardiness prevented me from doing so.

He came into my apartment talking a mile a minute into his Bluetooth, ignoring the angry look on my face. He'd left the door wide open. I don't know who this nigga thought he was.

Right before he got there, A'Jhani had thrown up on my chest and work vest. I'm not sure what was going on with him as he had no sign of fever or other cold-like symptoms, but I needed to change. I closed the door to the apartment and stood glaring at him like he'd lost his mind.

Ahmad held up his index finger and kept talking on his

Bluetooth for five more minutes. When he was finished he smiled at me. "You ready to go?"

"Ahmad, you're late. Forty-five minutes late to be exact. I missed my damn bus. I am not trying to get fired on my first day. I need this job, the bills are adding up. You will need to drop me off."

"I am sorry. My meeting ran over. So we finna load both kids into the car? I only got one booster seat." He looked down on me.

"That's fine. Rae'Jon's daycare is literally down the street. But I gotta take a two minute shower and throw on some new scrubs. I'll be back in less than five minutes."

I hurried from the room and into the bathroom where I already had the change of clothes on top of the sink. I stripped quickly and jumped into the shower. "Damn, I don't wanna be late."

Thankfully Ahmad was going to drive me so I would hopefully get there on time. His driving would save me thirty minutes. At this time I still had forty minutes to get there.

The shower water was just beading onto my shoulders when Ahmad stepped into the bathroom and pulled the curtains back. I covered my chest. He looked me up and down hungrily and gripped his piece through his pants.

"Damn, I'm a li'l sweaty, too. I need to take a quick shower before we hit the road." He stripped then got in behind me. Slowly, he took a hold of my waist and pulled me toward him. I could feel his erection poking into by backside.

I slapped at his hands. "Get off of me, Ahmad. Stop. This ain't happening. Stop. Please." I tried to turn around but he forced me against the wall and held my hip tightly. He took his piece and searched for my opening.

I elbowed him as hard as I could. "That's how you gon' play me? Really? Stop playing wit' me. You my ma'fuckin B.M. I can fuck this pussy whenever I want to." He kicked my legs apart and slammed into me hard.

I screamed as I dug my nails into his skin. "Get off of me! Please don't do this."

"Oh, really!" He pulled me back into him and began to take what he wanted aggressively. "This my pussy! Mine!" Harder and harder.

A lone tear sailed down my cheek as I tried to break his hold but it was of no use. He kept doing his thang. He was stronger. He was determined. I was weak. I was forced to submit to his assault.

BOOM! There was a split second of silence with the exception of his grunting behind me. Then A'Jhani began to scream at the top of his lungs. Ahmad continued to pump until he spew his seed, only then did he release me.

I jumped out of the shower and raced into the bedroom. A'Jhani had fallen off of the bed that Ahmad had negligently placed him on. He'd bumped his head on the hardwood floor. I scooped him up with Ahmad's seed running down my thighs. Not only had he'd just raped me, but he'd placed A'Jhani in danger by his careless acts of selfishness.

Ahmad came into the bedroom. He looked concerned. "Damn, what happened?"

"You were supposed to be out here watching him. Not trying to fuck me! Get out. Now!" I screamed. This made A'Jhani cry louder.

"What happened, li'l man?" He ignored me and stepped up to us. He grabbed A'Jhani out of my arms, but I kept my arms around him. "Man, let me see him, Jelissa."

"No, leave my house. This would not have happened had you been out here with him."

"Well, I told Rae'Jon to watch him."

"Ahmad, Rae'Jon is three-years-old! He is a child. That wasn't his responsibility. I specifically told *you* to keep an eye on them so I could shower. You were too busy tryna get some."

"He's okay, Jelissa. Ain't that right, li'l man?" Ahmad snuggled A'Jhani close to his chest, covering his face in kisses.

"Ahmad, just please go."

"Alright. Lemme just drop y'all off. I'll leave you be. Lemme just drop y'all off so I can be sure that my son is alright."

~

On the fourth of July of two thousand and fourteen, Wendella invited me to her Fourth of July celebration. I had done the best that I could to keep my distance from Ahmad with the exceptions of drop-offs and pickups.

Though her grandson and I were on terrible terms, I still loved Wendella and enjoyed her company. She'd promised me that Ahmad would not be there, and I trusted that.

I had reduced myself to staying inside of my apartment caring for my children. I didn't want to be around anybody, not even Jennifer because I felt so empty and broken inside, especially after the rape.

I had missed Wendella, and after some thought, I figured that a nice celebration would be a sure way to ease some of my sadness and gloom. It was Ahmad's week to have A'Jhani, so it would just be Rae'Jon and I.

When I arrived at Wendella's home at one o'clock in the afternoon, I was devastated to find that Ahmad was already there, present with both A'Jhani and his rumored fiancée, Brenda. I was flabbergasted. Not solely because of the fact that Ahmad was there but that Brenda was present, holding and kissing all over A'Jhani as if she were his mother.

I grew angry right away, but I was forced to keep my composure. I didn't want to come off as jaded, or petty.

It took all of the willpower I had inside of me to try and enjoy the summer get together, and no matter how hard I tried, I couldn't shake the fact that this broad was parading my son around as if he were her kid.

Ahmad had been sending me message after message trying to get back with me. He sent me slow songs that he swore spoke to our testament. He wrote poems. He did everything that he could to get into my good graces and I wasn't giving him anything.

When he saw me at the party he would only smile and hold Brenda closer to his body. She was sporting a new diamond engagement ring that looked as if he'd dropped a bag for it.

Finally, after watching them parade around for three hours I couldn't take no more. I walked in their direction and found a way to strategically get my son in my possession. I didn't give a damn if it was Ahmad's time. I was tired of that bitch playing house with my kid not knowing that Ahmad used to come over to my place and do the same shit.

"We need to talk." I stated to Brenda as I retrieved my child from her.

"About what?" She asked.

"Don't worry about. Just know I have something to show you." I smiled a devilish grin.

With my children in tow, I crept upstairs to Wendella's place and settled on her couch with A'Jhani in my lap. He was due for a feeding anyway. My head was hurting and Rae'Jon wanted to get out of the sun as well.

I couldn't have been upstairs for more than fifteen minutes when Brenda came up there right behind me. "So, you said we needed to talk?"

"Yes, I did."

"Can I ask about what?" Brenda took a seat on the couch across from me.

I couldn't lie, she wasn't a bad looking woman. She looked

like she could have been India Arie's twin. Same skin complexion, same physical makeup from head to toe, and had dreadlocks down her back. All that shit Ahmad had spoken about dating black women and he was engaged to married one. Was I not good enough to be a wife?

My blood began to boil. Damn, right I was jealous. This fool was really playin' with my mind. "*Your* man. I think you should know *your* man ain't who he claiming to be."

"What do you mean by that?"

"While y'all playin' happy family over here, he does the same mess at my house. We've been sleepin' together on and off since our son has been born. He claims he's only with you for the money and to maintain his image within the community."

She snickered. "How could he possibly have time to be with you when he's always working, in meetings and at our business office?"

I pulled out my phone. "That's what he might be telling you but this is what he's been telling me every day all day."

I showed her the phone and literally took her through every text message Ahmad had written me. I even showed her the ones where he was saying the only reason he was with her was because of her money and status. The more she read the more noises she made. I couldn't tell if she was shocked or angry. She got up off of the couch and handed the phone back to me. She left out of the apartment without saying another word.

Yea, it was wrong for me to rain on her parade but I no longer gave a damn. I was tired of being played for a fool. She was about look just as stupid as I'd been looking all these months.

I pulled out a baby wipe and began to wipe away her kisses from A'Jhani's face. Rae'Jon stood up and came over to see his little brother. He stood on his tippy toes to get a better view of him. I leaned A'Jhani down, and Rae'Jon kissed him.

Ahmad came through the door. He threw it open. "You lying ass bitch!" He closed the distance between us before I could do anything and yanked me up so hard that I dropped A'Jhani on the glass coffee table and he threw me across the room. Ahmad grabbed me by the throat and shook me, then delivered punch after punch, pulling my hair like a girl. "Bitch, I should kill yo' stupid ass."

Wendella came inside of the apartment. "What is going on in here?" She looked around in a panic.

Ahmad picked up a screaming A'Jhani. "This bitch lying on me. She just mad because I don't wanna fuck with her skinny ass."

I was broke up. I was in utter shock that I couldn't form a tear. I scooted over to Rae'Jon and hugged him to my body. He was crying and telling Ahmad to leave me alone. To stop beating up his mommy.

"Shut up, li'l punk ass boy." Ahmad jumped at Rae'Jon like he wanted to hit him.

"Ahmad, just go. Get out of here." Wendella urged, "my neighbors gone call the cops on all of y'all."

Both Ahmad and Brenda cursed me out. Then Wendella and Brenda got into it because Brenda wanted to attack me. Wendella stopped her. Ahmad called his grandmother out of her name for the simple fact of her trying to protect me. They began to argue with each other until Ahmad threatened to kill me for the fiftieth time. "You better watch yo' back, bitch." He warned. Then he left, taking A'Jhani with him.

As soon as he left, I called the police. I was sure he was going to kidnap our child, and follow through with his threats to kill me, or to have me killed. I needed protection. While Wendella's line was ringing for the 911 dispatcher, T.J. was calling me on my cellphone as if he could hear my prayers for protection. I picked it up right away crying my eyes out. Before he could say a word I told him everything that happened.

He paused for a second. "Fuck! Them niggas always doing that shit to the black women, never them snow bunnies though. That's some bullshit."

"So, what should I do? I'm scared." I was shaking uncontrollably.

He was quiet for a long while again. "Man sis, do what you gotta do to protect yourself and those babies. Fuck bruh right now. I ain't wit that rat shit but he playin' pussy. Do what you gotta do and tell that nigga I told you to since ain't nobody else trying to protect you. Then come and see me a-sap. I'm finna cop you a whip and send you some bread to get by. You hear me?"

I nodded, though I was confused as to how he was going to do all of that. "I hear you."

"I love you, sis."

"Thank you, T.J. I love you, too."

CHAPTER 6

NO PLACE QUITE LIKE HERE

I find myself reading old text messages when I'm bored
We find ourselves sexting 'til that connection is restored
I know that sounds immature, but if we never grow up
Then I wish you good luck on the seas that's inside this wall

I don't know how T.J. was able to do it but somehow he was able to send me eighty-five hundred dollars a few days after the fourth of July incident. I used a portion of the money to buy a used car that was in mint condition, and the rest to catch up on bills. The funds were a life saver, and a reason for me to take him seriously.

Two weeks after the fourth of July, Ahmad was arrested for parole violation. His probation officer didn't take to kindly to his assault of me, especially while my children were present. During the revocation hearing, Ahmad did all that he could to make me out to be the bad guy. He blamed the assault on me and said that it only took place because I was jealous of his new relationship. I laughed at that and was thankful that I wouldn't have to put up with him for eight months.

A month later, T.J. and I were fully in tune. The facility he was at allowed for them to have the phones from eight o'clock in the morning until eight o'clock at night with just a few breaks in between where they couldn't use the phone because of count and meal time.

He and I took advantage of this privilege. We talked on the phone at least five hours a day every day getting to know each other in a way that I had never gotten the chance to know any other man in my life. He shared so many secrets with me that blew my mind. And after a while, I found myself doing the same with him.

He wrote me long twenty plus page letters about how special I was, and my worth. He helped me to see myself in a new light. He taught me the true meaning of a man, and the importance of a woman's strength. He helped me to understand the rules of the game when it came to dating and surviving in a heartless world. He was brutally honest about everything. He refused to hold back any punches, and he took time to cater to my emotions. This I appreciated because I had always been an extremely emotional person.

Before I'd had the opportunity to seriously get to know him, all I had to go off of was what I knew about him through his family. I knew that he had one son. He spent a lot of time with Ahmad and every time I saw his son, he was well mannered and well dressed.

In addition to the things I'd heard about him, I'd learned that when he was on the streets he was a straight savage with a quick temper and extremely trigger happy when it came to gun play. He hated men and protected women, especially those in his family. All of the women in his family adored him.

After talking to him consistently on the phone for two months ,I was finally ready to see him. I had been loosely seeing Rae'Jon's sperm donor trying to give him a chance to get things right, but after so many games, his laziness, and inability to advance behind smoking skinny blunts, and popping pills, T.J. demanded that I kick him to the curb. And I did just that.

*I*t was August twenty-third of two thousand and fifteen when I finally got up the nerve to visit T.J. I'd been nervous for an entire twenty four hours prior. The night before, I'd groomed myself from head to toe. My hair was freshly done, so were my nails, and even though I was unsure as to what was set to take place I had even shaved Ms. Kitty. I felt both guilty and a little devilish in doing this. I had to come prim and proper.

The next morning, I had dropped my children off with their God mother and I was off to see him, shaking the entire way.

I had a million thoughts going through my mind. Would he like what he saw in person? Was I too skinny? Would they let me in to see him? Would he compare me to his son's mother? Would he look down on me because I had a child with his brother? And where were trying to take things, was it appropriate?" I was forced to shake all of the jitters off of me by the time I got to the prison.

It was huge. It looked like a big castle with barbwire around it. There were multiple guard towers with armed security inside of them. At the entrance, there was a line of people waiting to get inside. I sat in my car for a moment trying to collect my thoughts. After taking another ten minutes I got out and made my way inside.

I read all the signs that adorned the walls. Me being thorough and having watched too much damn TV, I had researched the prison to get an understanding of the rules and how things went for visitation. I found the dress code, the visiting hours, count clearance as well as the facility's DO's and DON'Ts.

When I walked into the building, I was stared down by so

many of the female visitors. I felt so out of place and small in a lobby full of people. It was similar to the feeling you got when people from a certain town *know you* were not from there. I was ready to turn around and go back home, but I pushed forward.

I approached the check in counter with my I.D. and visiting slip, placed it next to the line of others, about twenty slips before mine and went to take a seat until I was called. I observed women taking off their bras in the lobby as opposed to going into the bathroom in order to hurry up and get through the metal detector, crying babies not wanting to walk through the metal detector, visitors driving from two hours away being denied simply because their address on the I.D. didn't match the address in the system, visitors cussing the staff out, just complete and utter chaos.

After thirty minutes, my name was called. All my jewelry had been taken off, I had worn the proper bra, a peach-pink asymmetrical skirt with a black blouse to avoid any secretive clothing metals and I had my vending machine change ready. I didn't come to play nor did have time. It was important to always do your own research before going to an unknown place so that you were aware of what you were getting yourself into.

I walked through that metal detector effortlessly. I was handed a visiting slip with his and my name on it and carried it through a series of metal double doors. When I got inside of the visiting room, I took the paper up the officer and he looked it over before assigning me to a table.

I slowly made my way through the crowded room towards our assigned table. The room was packed with kids running around, omen of all shades and shapes adjusting their weaves and clothing, pushing up their breasts to put them on full display as best they could, fans blowing circulating nothing but hot air, men in all greens just staring at me.

I immediately became lightheaded, realizing that

somehow I had forgotten to eat because I was so fixated on seeing this man for the first time. So, I headed to the back of the visiting area towards the vending machines and purchased me a strawberry Pop tart, then made my way back to my seat.

I continued to observe my surroundings, eating my Pop Tart as a tall, baldheaded man of about six feet two inches with muscles bulging out of his greens came walking towards my direction. The man was gorgeous. His honey brown complexion was nicely oiled. He had thick eyebrows, thick kissable lips and a neatly shaped goatee. *I know T.J. ass better be just as fine. I never knew fine men existed here,* I thought to myself.

Once the man got closer, our eyes locked. He smiled giving me both shots of his deep dimples.

Please don't be heading in my direction. Please. I am already here to see someone. I was so nervous that I stayed seated eating my Pop Tart like he wasn't walking over to me.

"Man, you better get yo li'l fine ass up and gimme my kiss. Why you still sitting down?" He asked me.

This can't be T.J. The pictures he'd sent months prior looked nothing like the man that was standing before me now. I stood up mid chew. "Dang, my bad." *Did he just say kiss? Are we there yet?*

He grabbed me by my waist possessively and pulled me to him. His thick lips kissed mine ever so softly at first, and then he was more demanding, more hungrily. He groaned as he held me tighter. We both moaned as we melted into each other, me melting into his big arms.

When he broke our kiss, he took a step back and looked me up and down. "Damn, you bad. I knew you was fine and all that, but damn you cold." He kissed my lips again. "Come on, I set up some shit up back here so we can really chill. I been feenin' for yo' li'l fine ass for three years now." He took my hand and a guard waved us over.

"Um, where are we going?" I questioned, my anxiety getting the best of me.

"You can trust me. You know if ain't nobody else got you, I do." He continued to guide us to the back through a set of doors. Once there, the guard took us down a dimly lit hallway and stepped aside so we could enter into a room. We went inside of it and I looked up at T.J.

"T.J., all I can give you is forty-five minutes. That's shift change. Hurry up." The guard said. He got ready to leave.

T.J. grabbed his wrist. "Wait, for a whole ass gee, man fuck that." He looked like he was ready to blow.

The guard put up two hands to calm him. "Look, next week, tell her to come earlier, and I'll give you two an hour. Now go, you're down to forty minutes now." He stepped out of the room and locked the door. He turned off the light in the hallway, and I was spooked.

T.J. stepped in front of me. "Baby, are you nervous? I know we was hinting around all of this on the phone on some flirty shit, but we don't have to. I mean if you ain't ready." He kissed my forehead.

Hell no, I ain't ready. I have only known you through phone calls and letters. But then again, I haven't had any in almost a year. He smells so damn good though. Jelissa, this is Ahmad's brother, come on. This can't happen. I know, but he so fine. What if I look but don't touch? No, Jelissa. Kissing was enough. Damn, I got with the wrong brother. The fuck was I thinking.

His chest muscles were popping out of his shirt, and over the last few months, our connection was like none that I had ever known. I wanted him just as bad as he wanted me, but was it right though? I didn't care. "I'm ready." My mind spoke before my heart could.

T.J. sat me back on the bed. He knelt in front of me and started to kissing my toes after removing my sandals. I shuddered and closed my eyes. His lips felt like magic as they traveled all over my body. When he pulled my skirt up my thighs and moved my knees apart I moaned. *Damn, I am so glad I shaved.* My hairless sex lips were on full display. If we hadn't already crossed the line before, now we really had. He kissed my lips softly. He moaned into the apex of my thighs.

"Damn, you smell so good." He opened my petals and licked up and down my groove. His tongue made circles around my clitoris. When he sucked on it I shivered, damn near losing my mind.

He palmed my backside in his big hands and feasted on me as if he'd been starving. His tongue shot in and out of my pussy until I dug my nails into his shoulder blades and came so hard stuffing his face into my middle. He kept kissing and licking until I pushed him away. "You're so perfect. How could any nigga not cherish this diamond?"

He stood up with his dick poking against his green pants. I was still shivering when I reached to unzip him. I got his belt loose and his pants fell. I pulled down his boxers and became intimidated at the sight of his piece. Not only was it thicker than any I had ever seen before, but it was just as long. I tried to wrap my little hand around it but failed to do so. I stroked him with both hands.

"T.J., what do you think you about to do with this? You are not about to stretch me like that." I said looking up at him. The more I stroked his dick, the bigger it got.

"Baby, we gon' try to figure somethin' out. I gotta have some of you. You're all I been thinking about." He pulled me up and picked me up into the air as if I was light as a feather. My thighs instinctively wrapped around him. As soon as they did, he bit into my neck. He gripped his dick and searched for my hole. I felt his tip and I slid down with ease.

"Uhhhh! Wait." I groaned, feeling myself being stretched open.

He paused with me in midair. "You want me to stop baby, huh?" He lowered me back to the bed.

I dug my nails into his back. "No, just be gentle. Please. That's all I ask." I kissed his lips and sucked on them hungrily, disbelieving what I was doing.

"Okay, baby." He slowly eased into me until he sunk deep into my pussy. Then he pulled all the way out only to sink into me again. "I wanna fuck this pussy like a savage, Jelissa. I'm finna take you for myself anyway. I'll kill a ma'fucka over you and you know it."

He pulled back and slammed into me repeatedly. He sped up his motions. After only a few moments, he had my small frame balled up taking me down while he moaned into my ear how perfect I was. He went deeper and deeper with each stroke.

My nails dug deeper into the skin of his back. "Uhhhh! T.J.! Shit, baby. This so wrong. We so wrong. I'm yo' brother's baby mama!"

This made him fuck me like an animal. "Shit, Jelissa, don't say that. Don't say that." He was fucking me so hard and deep that I couldn't talk. I whimpered and came back to back on him.

He pulled out and bent me over the bed slamming into my pussy from behind. He held my hips and pounded me out. "I love you, boo! You my baby now! Just mine! Do you hear me?" He bit into my neck and came hard. I could feel his jets hitting my walls. He surprised me when he stayed hard and kept sexing me until we both came for a second time.

When it was all said and done, we both knew what it was and what it was going to be. We were both willing to face the backlash of this situation whenever it finally hit the fan.

"You were serious about marrying me?" T.J. asked.

"Were you serious about *wanting* to marry me?" I had a bad habit of answering a question with a question but that was me.

"Hell yeah. You are the first female I have ever thought about marriage with. And my brother didn't know what to do with you, but I'ma show him. That's my word."

∾

Visitation with T.J. lasted three hours and thirty minutes. I would be lying if I said it wasn't worth it. I did not want to leave him. I wasn't ready to return to the outside world once I got lost inside of T.J.

On my drive back, I immediately called Jennifer to tell her about my visit. The only thing I could think about was how I had had a baby with the wrong brother. This shit was mind blowing. Crazy part about all this was that I did not feel bad about it.

I had been holding off on T.J. meeting the boys but I was ready. I had a feeling that that situationship was only going to get deeper.

CHAPTER 7

FAMILY FIRST

These lips can't wait to taste your skin, baby, no, no
And these eyes, yeah, can't wait to see your grin, ooh ooh baby
Just let my love
Just let my love adorn you
Please baby, yeah

I will never forget how it felt the first time I took A'Jhani and Rae'Jon to see T.J. on our first family day visit. When we pulled up to the institution, the first thing my five-year-old son Rae'Jon said was, "Wow, Mommy, are we going into this castle? It looks cool." He looked up at the old dirty facility full of imagination.

"Yes baby, were going inside but I don't think it's going to look exactly how you are imagining it to look." I looked into the backseat to see if he heard me but he was already playing away on his tablet oblivious to the look of apprehension on my face.

Was I really about to do this? Could I really take my children inside of a prison? How could I be so sure that nothing would happen to them? After all, this was a place where they kept the most deadliest of human beings as well as predators. What if one of them snapped out and hurt one of my children? What could I do? What kind of mother would that make me?

I sat there for a long time trying to gather myself and get my mind right. My imagination began to run away with me for the negative. I couldn't do this. I wasn't ready to introduce my children to this side of my life. I started the car again, ready to pull off and go home when my phone rang. Looking at the face I was able to see that it was T.J. calling me. I trembled. How did he always know when to check in? I took a deep breath and closed my eyes. I allowed for the phone to ring a few times, before I answered it.

"Hello."

"Hey Baby girl, how far away are you? You already know I'm missing you like crazy, and I wanna meet our babies for the first time."

Our. Did he just say our babies? "Honey, I'm afraid to bring them in. What if they get hurt? I don't think I am ready to expose them to all of this."

"What! Man, I wish somebody would even come near our family. Baby, you already know that it ain't even like that here. You know how they honor ya man. These niggas ain't crazy, and I'm nuts over you. Those babies are a part of you which makes them a part of me. I want to see *my* kids. Come on in. Now, Precious."

Every time he called me Precious he made me feel so loved and protected. If I didn't come in to see him today then I wouldn't be eligible to visit again for three days. I couldn't be away from him that long. I needed my man just as much as he needed me. I trusted him. "Promise me nothing will happen to my babies."

"First of all, they are *our* babies. Secondly, you have my word that nobody will even come close to our sons. I put my life on that." He was quiet for a moment. "Now, please come in. I need to kiss those perfect lips and be with my Rib. It's been crazy the last few days without you."

"How so?" I loved when he often told me how difficult it had been to be away from me. For once in my life, aside from boys, I felt wanted. Needed.

"Baby, you are my life now. All I can think about is you every second of every day. Nothing makes sense unless it revolves around you. Now, I need you Li'l Mommas, only you."

I was smiling. "Okay, honey. Here I come."

"Bet, damn I appreciate you so much. Its yo fault you got me this damn crazy too. I'll see you in a minute. I love you."

"I love you, too." I sat there holding the phone in my left hand while I watched my precious children through the rear view mirror. Father Jehovah, please protect us and please make sure that I am making the right decisions. If you disapprove of this union Father give me a couple signs to let me know this day. However, if you approve please give me those signs as well. In Jesus Holy and precious name. Amen.

~

*S*eeing my children be searched as if they were common criminals was almost enough to make me turn around. Rae'Jon was one month into his fifth year, and A'Jhani was one month into his second year.

They were made to take off their little jackets first, and then two guards waved metal detector wands all over them as if they were smuggling something. After they were searched, and proven to not be dirty with contraband, it was my turn. I was made to go through the metal detector. It went off, so I went through again.

The guard, a tall, heavy set white man with a bald head warned me. "If it goes off again, you will not be permitted to see your visitor today, ma'am. Maybe you need to take off your bra." He eyed my chest solicitously and looked back into my eyes.

This gave me an eerie feeling. I stepped away from him and ushered the children into the bathroom where I removed my bra. After removing it, I felt so vulnerable. Once again, I thought about leaving. I began to replay T.J.'s last words over in my head for strength. After returning back to the metal detector, I held up the bra for the guard to see and placed it inside of the plastic cubby next to the metal detector. I kept my arms across my chest as I walked through the machine. Thankfully, it didn't go off.

I sighed in relief when the guard handed me the paperwork and told me to enjoy my visit.

~

As soon as T.J. walked into the visiting room, I ran to him and he picked me up, wrapping his arms around me. The visiting room was packed but I swear it felt like we were the only ones present. He held me in his big arms and kept me in the air for a full minute before he put me down and kissed my lips. He was tender, yet firm. His muscles tensed as he tongued me down. He took a step back and looked into my brown eyes. His eye brows furrowed.

"Baby, what's the matter?" He held the right side of my face ever so lovingly.

"They made me take my bra off, and the man was so obvious about his pervert ass interest. They treated the boys like thugs, and I just feel so degraded right now. But we're here." My eyes watered.

"Damn boo, I'm so sorry." He kissed my forehead. "I am so thankful for you, baby, I promise I am. I vow to make this day up to you. I owe you for doing this, do you understand me, Gorgeous?"

"Yes." I hugged his muscular frame again. I needed him to pay extra attention to me today. I felt violated. I felt like I was on an island with my children. The feelings going on inside of me at this time were almost indescribable.

T.J. held me a moment longer, and then knelt down in front of Rae'Jon. "What's good handsome man?"

Rae'Jon blushed. He hugged my leg and tried to ignore T.J. He looked up at me. I could see the fear in his eyes.

"It's okay, baby. You've talked to him on the phone remember? He's the one that bought you the Power Wheel, and all of those clothes and stuff. This is T.J."

"Hi T.J." Rae'Jon continued to hold me and responded by not looking up at T.J.

"What's good, li'l homey?" T.J. laughed. "And this must be A'Jhani?" He picked A'Jhani up and kissed his cheek. "I been wanting to meet you. How are you?"

A'Jhani had a pacifier in his mouth. He nodded and kept right on sucking on it. T.J. kissed his cheek and held him close to his heart. A'Jhani laughed and wrapped his little arms around T.J.'s neck. We all sat down with T.J. pulling my chair out for me. I had never met a man with as many manners as he had for me. His manners were another reason I knew he was for me. He always took time to make sure I was treated like a special lady.

T.J. kept A'Jhani with him on his lap as he and I held hands. The visiting room was once again crowded. There were children all over the place having the time of their lives. "They can go and play with the other children if you're cool with that?"

I wasn't. I still worried about the other inmates hurting my babies. "Nah, they good right here. Besides, don't you wanna get to know them better?"

"Well, this one," he said, pointing at A'Jhani, "I already know by DNA. I feel crazily connected to him just by holding him. He looks just like my momma" He kissed all over

A'Jhani's face, making him laugh. "But Rae'Jon, I need to get to know. Come here, Rae'Jon."

Rae'Jon got out of his seat and gingerly came over to him. He looked nervous. I could only imagine it was because he'd witnessed the abusive relationships that I'd had in the past prior to T.J., including the verbally abusive and destructive relationship that I'd had with his own biological father. He may have seen T.J. as one of those aggressors, or maybe he equated all men as being predators to his small mother because all of those of his past had been. Either way, T.J. picked him up, and sat him on his right knee.

"Listen Rae'Jon, I know that you and mommy have been through a lot, and it's going to take some time before you trust me, but I just want you to know that I love your mother with all of my heart, and I love you, too. I will never hurt her, you, or A'Jhani. I am here to protect all three of you, and to make sure that you never need for anything. Do you understand that?"

Rae'Jon nodded. "Yes."

"Good. Now, can I please have a big boy hug? You got all of those muscles for a reason." He opened his right arm wide while he held A'Jhani in his left.

Rae'Jon stood up and grunted while he hugged him trying to give him as much love strength as he could. After he grunted himself to exhaustion, he climbed on to T.J., and their relationship has become the strongest relationship that Rae'Jon has built with any man to this day.

A decision I'll never regret.

CHAPTER 8

YOUR SACRIFICE

> Some people they call me crazy
> For falling in love with you
> They can take me and lock me away baby
> 'Cause there is nothing those bars can do
> I will be the rising moon after setting sun
> Just to let you know that you'll always have someone
> I will be the clearest day when the rain is done
> So you will always know

*T*hings had been going so well between T.J. and me. The boys were warming up to him and we began to seriously talk about our future together. But I'll never forget the call that brought me to my knees. January 1st of two thousand and sixteen.

"Hello, may I speak with Ms Jelissa Williams, please?"

"This is she," I replied.

"Hello, Ms. Williams. My name is Sergeant Tonio Melly here at Waupun Correctional Institution."

"Yes..." my heart was pound in my chest. Oh Lord, Who did he fight now? My husband was a ticking time bomb ready to go off at any time and I knew incoming calls from the prison was never a good thing. Our goal had been to keep him focused and on his best behavior. The quicker he was home, the better.

"Uh yes, I just wanted to inform you of the incident that took place yesterday."

Incident? The hell he talking about, 'incident'? I tried as best I could to swallow the large lump in my throat. Dammit, T.J. We agreed no fighting. "Yes, sir. What happened?

"Mr. Edwards was stabbed sixteen times-" I dropped the phone before he could finish. I fell to my knees as tears burned my face. I opened my mouth but no words came out. Please, Lord. I finally found my better whole. Don't take him from me. Please.

I retrieved the phone from the floor, hands shaking. "Is he okay, Mr. Melly? Please tell me he's okay." I could barely form the words.

"Yes, ma'am, Mr. Edwards is okay though in critical condition. He'll be able to go into detail with you about the incident when he reaches out to you in about a week or so. We have him in the protective unit to keep a close eye on him. I just wanted to inform you."

"A week or so? Why can't I speak with him now?" I questioned, "he could have died."

"Ma'am, I understand your concerns, but I assure you, he is okay. I said a week being that he's in HSU so we can monitor his wounds. He'll be moved to a single cell room after a week and that is when he'll have access to the phones, twice a week for 30 minutes."

"This is ridiculous. When can I come see him?"

"In a week, ma'am once he's been transitioned to his room. Did you have any other questions for me?"

"No, thanks." I hung up the phone before he could respond.

I knew who did this. A week prior, I had been warned.

"Jelissa, stay away from him. He is not who you think he is. I am not mad at you. I am more upset with him. I am more upset with him and that nigga gotta pay for his sins. He know how this shit goes. Stay out of this. It's between him and I. Stay out of this." Ahmad lowered his eyes as he glared at me over the top of the car I had just loaded A'Jhani into after completing one of Ahmad and I's many child exchanges. "I'm telling you to be smart. It was already disclosed to me that you and he are messing around now. Is that true? I just looked at him. I didn't know want to say.

Ahmad continued, "The only reason I ain't gon' deal with you for this betrayal like I am with him is because you are the mother of my child, but I'm warning you, if you know what's good for you, you will back off." He got ready to sit in his car and stopped.

He snickered. "Besides, I raised him. I know how that fool really get down. He ain't no one woman man, and you ain't his type. Trust me on that. Whatever he's telling you is fake. Trust me on that. When he drove away, he left me stuck picking my face up off the ground.

Could he be telling the truth? Was it possible? Could T.J. be running game on me, and if so what could he possibly be looking to gain.

Up until this point, T.J. had done nothing but keep his word. He was meeting me more than halfway when it came to my bills and expenses. He was loving and consistent in the boys' lives. He'd sent me a copy of his visiting list where he'd cut off all of his visitor's with the exception of a few that *I* approved that were his blood family.

All other women had been removed for nearly a year. His phone times were consumed with me, and I took up every visit that he was allowed, so I don't know why was I allowing for Ahmad to manipulate my brain every now and then.

After I hung up the phone with the facility, I called Wendella and told her what had taken place. Instead of her expressing her concerns, she immediately began interrogating me. "When did you and T.J. start messing around? Honey, don't you know that he's Ahmad's half-brother? What's the matter with you?"

"Excuse me, Ms Wendella, but did you hear me say that your grandson has been stabbed sixteen times, and he's in serious condition?"

Tears were already falling down my small face. How could she not be terrified for him. He'd always made sure that she was well taken care of. This didn't make any sense.

"I heard you, and I don't give a damn. He ain't got no right doing that to Ahmad. They are brothers. He got what he got. One of my brothers killed the other over a woman. It's history repeating itself all over again. If something happens, that will weigh heavily on your conscious. I wish I could..."

I hung up the phone before she could mentally damage me some more. Was she right? Was this my fault? Should I release T.J. before something worse happened to him? Damn, I needed to hear his voice so bad. I was losing my mind. What if he died?

I started to cry harder. I stopped and called around to all of his family. Each person gave me an attitude equivalent to that of Wendella. One of his cousins swore to kick my butt when she saw me. I hung up on one person after the next until I found myself lonely, and grief stricken. It would be an entire week before I could hear his voice and the phone call would only last for ten minutes.

When the phone finally rang, and I saw that it was T.J. calling. I had been cooking dinner for the children. I turned down the eye on the stove and rushed to accept the call. "Honey, are you okay?"

T.J. groaned into the phone. He took a second that felt like an eternity. "Baby, I'm good. They can't kill a solider. I told you I will never leave you, girl. I am missing you like crazy."

I was already crying. "Baby, I know who did this."

"I do too, and I'ts all good. I don't give a fuck what that nigga try. I love you. He gon' have to literally kill me to keep me away from you and our little family.

In the Bible, God always made those that he entered into a covenant with, shed blood before the covenant was reached. I knew these niggas were coming, and I was willing to shed blood for you so that we could enter into this eternal covenant with each other and God. Now that I have, we gotta get baptized, and then married before I get home.

All I see, and all I wanna be with is you. Fuck the world. Word to God." He was quiet for a second. "So, are you going to be my wife if I can put that rock on yo' finger? I need you to be my wife, Jelissa. I promise to elevate us on every level, starting with our Faith. The Bible says to first seek the kingdom of God and all of His righteousness, and the rest will be added onto you. We gotta seek and submit to Jehovah first, and then we will overcome our many struggles and enemies.

"You have one minute left to talk." Came the recording.

"Noooo!" I had so many questions for him. I needed to know if he was safe? Was his injuries healing? When I could visit? How did they catch him? Was more drama pending? T.J. had an assaultive history when it came to other inmates. He didn't like men at all. I knew revenge was on his mind but I needed him home. Trouble was a detriment to our family.

"Yo boo, I love you, Baby girl. You are my everything. I'll die for you. I am your sacrifice. I mean that."

"Honey, I need you. I love you so much." I cried falling to my knees. The phone clicked off, and I broke down.

To this day, I am not quite sure how T.J. and I managed to make it through that incident. He does have lifelong injuries as a result of his stabbing. I am just grateful to God that I still had him.

When asked would he have done anything differently way back then, his answer is always the same, "No Bubbie, I'd do it all again."

CHAPTER 9

SOMETIMES LOVE IS NOT ENOUGH

I care about you, baby, baby
More than you'll ever know
More than you'll ever know
Please do not drive me crazy, crazy
Unless you're gonna go with me
No pressure
No pressure, I know you're real
The pressure
The pressure will make you feel

In 2017, our reality had finally set it. We were married and had to start thinking of ways to advance our family.

One of the hardest things for me to face was the fact that no matter how I loved T.J., love just wasn't enough to pay the bills.

Being involved in a serious relationship with a man that was behind the wall meant that there were so many things that you had to pay for just to function. It started with the phone.

Communication between us was important so the phone was essential. But the phone like so many other things costed money, often times money that you don't have.

It got to a point where T.J. and I had become so addicted to one another that we were spending an average of eight hundred dollars a month on the phone alone, and this was the minimum amount. Sometimes the bill would get as high as twelve hundred if we were really in need of each other's love and guidance.

In addition to the phone, was gas and car maintenance expenses. I was driving an hour to get to him, and an hour to get back home, four days a week every week for five years straight with no weeks off. This took a lot of time, money and energy. Then when I got there I had to have money for the vending machines so we could eat as a family because this was as close as we could come to a family dinner at this time.

The vending machine was highway robbery. The cheapest item was a dollar twenty five, and that was a bag of potato chips which it took two of them to make Rae'Jon happy. The sandwiches were five dollars, and the soda pops were two dollars. We averaged forty dollars for each visit. That was a hundred-sixty dollars each week and six hundred-forty dollars a month. Along with the prison bills, I still had to pay rent, car note, insurance, energy, water, clothes, child care, and food bills. I was miserable, and T.J. told me a million times before that a lesser woman would crumble under my circumstances.

Now I had to give it to him, my husband had always been a dope boy at heart. A hustler. He refused to allow me to struggle, especially on his account, so he went into super hustle mode once he decided to take upon the load of father and husband to our family.

He would send me a thousand dollars at a time, or have me going to Western Union where money would be waiting for me once I gave the people my information and my ID. He took the bills personal and didn't allow for me to send him any money until all of them were paid and I had some for myself.

After times like this I would feel enamored. He'd call and all I would want to talk about was us, and our love for each other. He would express his love briefly, before he was redirecting the conversation to business, and the next month's bout of bills. This often led to arguments because I didn't want to always focus on next month when we'd recently accomplished all of our financial obligations for the month that we were in.

I needed that emotional connection when the physical was limited. Don't get me wrong, I loved having a man who was ambitious and about his business. He refused to allow his circumstances to make excuses as to why he couldn't be the man
I needed.

There were often days when the love aspect of our relationship was completely disregarded. It was all business. It was as if my husband had a hard time splitting the hairs.

This was going to definitely become a major concern for me once he was home. Though I understood his need to provide, I needed us to find a happy medium. I didn't want work to take precedence over our marriage and that's where we were heading.

I was a praying woman, but at that time I wasn't trying to hear nothing about my Faith.

CHAPTER 10

BORN AGAIN

Change me, oh God
Make me more like you
Change me, oh God
Wash me through and through
Create in me a clean heart
So that I may worship you

I will never forget the day when those magical words came out of T.J.'s mouth. "Baby, it's time that we get baptized. I been reading the Word like crazy, and from what I read, I feel like the only way we are going to be able to get all of the blessings that Jehovah has for us is if we go under that water and come up with a new spirit and body. What do you think?"

Prior to this phone call, he and I had been arguing a lot about our different needs when it came to each other. If it were up to T.J., every time I came to see him he would find a way to pay so that we could do our sexual thing but about four months into out seeing each other that had been shut down majorly, and we were reduced to phone sex.

T.J. was used to us being together in the physical, but after that was no longer an option the phone thing became an obsession for him. Whenever he heard my voice, he was ready to go and on most occasions so was I.

But then there were times when I didn't want us to report to the sexual side of things. I wanted things to be strictly emotional.

Women are wired differently than men. We are emotional creatures whereas men are physical. There were many days where T.J. just couldn't go there emotionally. The daily frustrations of being incarcerated would get the best of him and the only way to break that was for us to resort to sex.

We argued about this concept daily. I didn't understand how men expected women to just strip down and be ready to go without any foreplay. And that was the emotions for me. Foreplay.

"Why do I always have to submit to your needs first when I have needs too?" He'd argue.

"The same way in which I'd submit and cater to what you need something. It doesn't matter if I am not in the mental space to get physical with you. I still try because I know that's what you need. But you have to do the same for me."

It was a back and forth battle, constantly. He didn't have an issue catering to me, but there were moments when he just couldn't. He never had a problem with doing his part as long as it led to our phone sex, but on the days where it was solely emotional bonding and no sex, were the days that we argued.

This ultimately became draining and led to a sudden disconnect, and before you knew it, all kinds of crazy thoughts were going through my mind as well as his. Thoughts that would have shattered our relationship if we'd ever taken part in them.

There were many times I questioned whether or not I was

capable of being the woman he needed, questioning if I could really hold him down year after year, questioning whether he really loved me or not and really wondering if this marriage was really worth putting my life on hold.

I don't think he truly understood the position I was put in when we got together. Yes, I understood what I was getting myself into as far as waiting, but I don't think I fully comprehended what it all entailed.

I was always asked, *how do you do it? If it was me, I would have not been able to do it. Do you think he's really going to be faithful to you when he gets home?*

These were the type of questions that made a woman like me in my position really think, especially during times where he and I weren't seeing eye to eye.

There's was a movie that I watched that changed my way of thinking forever. I think it might have saved us from self-destruction before we even really had the chance to see the full potential in our marriage.

It was War Room. After watching that movie, I knew then that I wanted and desired more than anything to give my life over to Christ. I knew that If T.J. and I had any chance of our marriage surviving after his bid, we needed a new perspective from the heavenly places.

T.J. and I were baptized together around the same time on March 13th in two thousand and sixteen. It gave me hope to see him just as serious about our marriage as I was. It gave me the strength to continue and push forward despite the thoughts of doubt that consumed my mind.

I went to work that night. I found a spare closet in my home, cleared it out and spent day and night in there. I prayed, cried, begged, laughed, pleaded, slept and sat still just to exist. There were days when prayer just wasn't enough. I felt like it wasn't working and I needed more. I needed right-now type answers. I remained consistent and held onto my faith.

CHAPTER 11

EMPTY BED

Gotta get this paper, get this cake up
Gotta do my hair, gotta put on makeup
Gotta act like I care about this fake stuff
Straight up, what a waste of my day
If I had it my way
I'd roll out of bed
Say 'bout 2:30 mid-day

One of the hardest parts I struggled with was leaving our visits almost every day and returning home to an empty home as well as an empty bed. As the winter months approached, it became harder and harder to leave him. Most days, I didn't want to visit for this reason alone.

During the winter, I always went through strong bouts of depression and I just couldn't shake myself free from mind. I was literally drowning. There were times T.J. knew exactly what to say and days when his words would shatter me. "Why are you sad? You have no reason to be sad? You gotta take yourself up outta that or you risk bringing those around you down as well."

Newsflash, depression was never something to take yourself up out of. There was never a *reason* to be depressed. You could never control when that cloud of darkness hovered over you. I wonder how he'd feel if he knew of all the times I'd cried before entering the visiting room or right after. The times I cried needing him to be strong for me when I couldn't be that for myself.

It didn't matter how much you loved a man, or how devoted and dedicated you were to him, that empty bed would always be a nightly obstacle that you were forced to overcome. That along with the naysayers. And trust me, there were plenty negative nancies. So many people will hate on you for the life you have, yet they don't know how hard it is to manage.

Queens, to this day, I cannot tell you how I managed to keep strong year after year. I was ready to walk away so many times, and I mean many, *many* times. I am proud of these most but I am human. My way of protecting myself from being hurt was to always walk or run away. Over the years, I have learned how to probably cope as running away from problems never results in a positive solution or a solution period.

But I encourage those in my current position to keep fighting, especially if you know you have a good man. And to understand that God will never allow for you to travel down a road like this unless He knew the extent of your many blessings on the other end that are waiting on you.

When you grow weary, lay your burdens down on to Him and beg Him for rest and guidance. I can't count how many times I begged for rest.

CHAPTER 12

A GODLY MARRIAGE

So every time I think of her I'm thanking you
And when I give my love to her I'm thanking you
Loving her like Christ love the church cuz you told me too
Yeah she help me see all your glory
Sometimes I don't feel like I'm worthy
But I'm under your covenant so I ain't worried
I'm just thanking you

My grandmother always told me that prayer and having faith in God would move mountains in any situation. I had always wanted to believe this, but it surely did take me a long time to see this as truth.

It was a few years into our relationship when T.J. and I started spending hours on the phone praying with each other and reading the Bible. As T.J. started studying his word and at my advisement, staying away from the underworld of the prison where he was familiar with hustling and doing whatever it took to make it happen for his family, money was scarce.

This meant that all of the costs fell onto my shoulders, and to say that I wasn't close to breaking down would be a lie. It seemed like the more we prayed and read the Bible, the worse our situation became.

I was still going through hell when it came to Ahmad and co-parenting with him, but I was thankful that a restraining order was in place although he found other ways to come at me either through his family or friends.

T.J. was also forced to deal with all sorts of impossible things inside of the prison that he refused to disclose to me about because he knew I would only worry about him.

With the bills adding up, and me falling behind, yet still supporting him as best as I could, I found myself evicted and put out on the street. I was forced to move back in with my dad until I got on my feet.

Even though we may have hit our lowest point we found way to love each other harder and we kept our faith in Jehovah giving him ten percent of everything we had any time we got a hold of any funds. This was hard because when you have a hundred percent of barely anything, giving up ten percent of that is nearly impossible, but we did, and we kept praying and remaining steadfast in his Word amongst the pressure of the world.

Then on April twentieth of two thousand and seventeen, after submitting ten manuscripts to Lockdown Publications, I received a call from the C.O.O. Shawn Walker, saying that the company was interested in our manuscripts.

The opportunity to become a published Author didn't become real until hubby and I signed a contract. I couldn't believe it. T.J. and I had worked so hard with writing our stories and it seemed like it was finally paying off. It was then that T.J. and I knew that the lives of our family would forever be changed for the better.

CHAPTER 13

BALANCING ACT

I'm not okay, no, I'm not okay
I'm not okay
Losing my faith, I'm losing my faith
Slipping away, you're slipping away
I'm not okay, no, I'm not okay
I'm not okay

The love my husband and I share is undeniable. Those who have had a chance to get to know us and follow our story know this as well. But we've had many downs just like every couple on our journey. The biggest battle that took us a while to overcome was him understanding the many hats I had to wear.

I think my husband or any incarcerated person for that matter, honestly forgets or refuses to understand how our days (those of us who are free) are different than theirs. The days may seem longer to them but the days for us on the outside just fly by.

I have been to jail once in my twenty-nine years of living,

for twenty-four hours due to a minor altercation with my sister. For that short time, those hours felt like years. Those hours dragged, so while I could understand how my husband expected me to get so much done, it was not feasible.

The many hats I had to switch between was being a mother, a full-time student, a full-time employee, an author and wife, visiting my husband four times a week while he was at his old facility.

Visiting days were literally an all-day process. Those who have incarcerated loved ones can definitely relate. It took me an hour to get to T.J. and visits lasted three hours and thirty minutes. I never missed a visit. Didn't matter if I was sick, tired, suffering from migraines that blurred my vision, sick kids, etc T.J. was not trying to hear it. He had got so accustomed to and spoiled with the visits that asking for a day off from visiting to simply rest often led to arguments.

So I was often only left with *three days* out of each week to handle any business related to our books, be a mom, household worker, student, etc. On top of all these things, my husband expected me to complete *his* editing/formatting/proofreading projects within a week being that it only took him about a week to write a full 45,000 word novel. His logic was that since it took him a week to write, I only needed a week to edit and proofread. The expectations he often placed on me weren't fair.

I was honestly struggling to keep it together most days. Crying myself to sleep, being distance or even too emotional. Often times, I questioned his love for me as we'd sit in front of one another. He'd see the tiredness in my face and body and not once did ever dawn on him to give me rest. To offer me something. To be considerate of what I needed. That type of wear and tear on a person often broken them and pushed them away.

At that point in our marriage, I started to resent him and visitation become more of a chore and obligation as opposed to a time of enjoyment for me. Eventually, he started to pick up on that energy and he'd say some irritating shit that'd set me off. "When I am able to transfer to my next facility it'll be better. I'll be in low level custody which means more freedom. More stuff to do. I'll be able to do more and I won't need you as much. You'll be able to rest and have time to yourself."

And as much as I needed rest physically, emotionally and mentally, the only thing I heard was, 'I won't need you as much'. I couldn't quite explain to him why hearing this hurt me so bad but it did.

It's like he had totally disregarded all the traveling I had to do every time they moved him from place to place. I was always from and center. No matter the distance. The last facility he was at before he was moved to a center was two hours and thirty minutes away, and I took that drive every week, *twice* a week. I don't know no woman that would have went through so many extremes for the man they loved.

As the years went on, I was given more time to indulge in self-care and think about me, but I still felt unfilled. I was still unhappy. I am sure it was because my "me-time" was forced due to circumstances. It wasn't given out of the kindness of my husband's heart. It wasn't him saying, "Baby Girl, you sound tired. Rest up today. I'll be okay. I want you to be okay." And that's what I craved more than anything.

~

As my husband was getting closer and closer to preparing for his homecoming, completing his last programs, his family members were coming out the woodworks, including his baby mama.

Ma'fuckas needed favors and wanted to visit all of a sudden, but not neow person was there when he was stabbed, damn near left for dead. Not one person offered money to ensure he was eating three meals minimum a day. Not one person called to just do a wellness check to make sure he was still breathing. That was all me. Li'l Jelissa carrying not only the weight of the world but the weight of a broken incarcerated man.

I refused to let anyone reap the benefits of the hard work I had to put in to keep this man sane and out of trouble, to get him where he was today.

Sometimes, T.J. often misunderstood my selfishness with him until I used the analogy of the childhood story, *The Little Red Hen*. I am sure you all are familiar with this story.

The Little Red Hen needed help baking bread but every *friend* she asked always had some sort of excuses. No one wanted to put the work in. But when it came time to enjoy the fruits of her labor, every one of those same *friends*, wanted to enjoy her bread as well and she wasn't having it.

I was the Little Red Hen. I literally put my all into T.J. He never needed for anything. He always had canteen every week, no less than $1,000 on his books, two pairs of brand new shoes every year, the newest devices the prison's allowed, a new wardrobe, and vitamins to maintain his health.

Every family member he needed, never showed up. There was always an excuse. But these were the same folks he paid the bills for from the *inside*. He helped them during their time of need but none of them reached for him.

I'd be damned if I allowed his family and so called friends to creep into his life, thinking they'd reap the benefits of a man *I* took the time to invest in and upgrade. Call me what you want, but I wasn't tolerating it.

CHAPTER 14

LOSING BUT FINDING ME

I'm free
I'm human but I'm comfortable with me
I'm capable, got everything I need
I'm focused and I'm living out my dreams
I feel
My family, their love surrounding me
There's nothing in this world I'd rather be
Than me
I'm free

As much as I hate to admit this part, over the years I had honestly lost myself within my marriage. I literally thought, breathed, ate and slept us.

I had isolated myself from everyone and everything. I had no life outside of him and the boys. Whatever he went through on the inside, I was going through out here. If he was confined to his cell, I was confined to my room. When the phones shut off for the night, my phone was off. I ate the same things he ate. It was as if I, myself was incarcerated.

Truthfully, I spent every waking moment, including holidays with T.J. We had created our own little world in which only our little family existed. We shut everyone and everything out. As he transitioned to lower security facilities, things started to change abruptly.

Soon enough, this came to bit us back in the butt especially when my depression had gotten the better of me as he was my only outlet. Everything about us that I had grew accustomed to had come to a halt. He was changing on me. He became less patient, easily frustrated and irritable as well as argumentative, yet I found myself desiring him more and more because he was literally all I had. This in turn ignited the insecurities that were still deeply embedded within me.

It came to a point where I was literally on the floor of my prayer closet one night, breaking down. We had had our last petty argument about the lack of love and affection between us.

Things went from sugar to shit real quick when the Corona Virus Pandemic took over and shut visits down. The last time we had seen one another was the day after my birthday. March 10th, 2021 would make it a year since we've had physical contact.

Jelissa, what's happening to you?

I was learning that the enemy will use the brokenness of your past to destroy your future. It was time for me to find myself. I started to dislike the woman I was becoming while with him. I no longer knew what it was that made Jelissa happy. His need to point out my flaws and not hold himself accountable when he was wrong started to frustrate me. I no longer wanted what I was being given.

I knew that change had to start with me. I learned that our relationships with ourselves set the tone for every other relationship we have in our lives and I knew that even at the age of twenty-nine, I was still struggling with loving myself and being comfortable in my own melanated skin.

I was seeking validation from my husband constantly. His words were like gold to me. But I knew I could no longer carry on like this. I didn't need a therapist nor anybody around to tell me what I already knew. I knew that our marriage was becoming unhealthy. For him and for me.

I had to learn Jelissa again. As I searched deep within myself, I found that there were things still inside of me that still needed healing and restoration. And the only way we heal it to acknowledge that we are hurting or we repeat what we don't repair.

So, I started with a letter to myself. I apologized to me for all of the things I had accepted in my past. I apologized to myself for neglecting me and placing every one else's needs before my own. I spoke life into me. I was doing the very things I expected everyone else to do for me.

I dove deeper into my faith where I discovered my spirituality. It was time for me to awaken myself spiritually. As I drew closer to God, I found the healing power in meditation, prayer, singing bowls and just the act of simply being. I had to learn the art of letting go and just living in the moment.

Spiritual awakening is hard though! I have learned that it is more than mantras, meditations, affirmations, alignment and higher elevation. It is a journey that requires you to do the shadow work, discovering who you truly are. You will go through many stages in which you are learning to experience and accept different levels of emotions, battle the darkness trying so hard to conquer you, recognize your toxic behaviors, hold yourself accountable, release your need to control, and set yourself free from all that was to welcome all that is and will be. To simply exist. Just know that spiritual awakening *is not* for the faint of heart.

CHAPTER 15

WHEN IT'S ALL SAID AND DONE

Please let me feel inner peace
From my center at the center of me
Please let me feel inner peace
From my center at the center of me
My heart is open
I am aware
In me is a knowing
Of love, love, love

My journey as a prison wife has been far from easy. If you follow me on social media, you would have had the chance to see the ups and downs I have shared. It has not been a straight road. My husband and I have had some serious trials and tribulations.

I think my husband will agree with me when I say that the secret that has been holding our marriage together has been God himself.

He's honestly been my saving grace during the times and

seasons where I never thought my husband and I would walk out of unscathed.

I have created a routine that helps me continue to promote healing and personal growth. Every morning, I drink a half 16 oz of bottled water, go make my tea, turn on meditation music and grab my affirmations and gratitude journal to write in.

The more I continue to work on myself, the more things change around me for the better.

While I don't know what the future holds for T.J. and me, I do know that I love my husband dearly. He has been my heaven on earth despite our ups and down. As long as we continue to put GOD first, there's no storm that'll come our way that we won't be able to weather.

It is so easy to get sucked into the life of another, especially your incarcerated loved one. All you want to do is rescue them. You can't excuse the fact that they made poor choices in the past.

God knows how to use people for His purposes. He knows how to bring about change in their lives and in their hearts. Trust in Him. Pray for your loved one. That is the most incredible act of love you can perform for them. Remember, *the Will of God will Not take You Where the Grace of God Will Not Protect You.*

PRAYER FOR MY PRISON WIVES/FAMILIES

Heavenly Father,

I am praying for every prison wife, girlfriend or loved one supporting their family members behind bars. Please cover and strengthen all of these relationships during this pandemic.

Thank you Lord for your protection thus far. We could not have made it this far without You. Thank you for your mercy, grace, unconditional love, and undeserved kindness. Please teach us how to love one another as defined by Your Word. We love You, Lord.

In Jesus Name, Amen!

THANK YOU

I would like to sincerely thank you all for taking the time to read about my journey as a Prisoner's wife. This journey has not been as easy as it seems. It was not an easy task being vulnerable and putting myself out there like that. I pray you enjoyed it.!

Please leave a review. I'd gladly appreciate it. Thank you all again! God bless!

ABOUT THE AUTHOR

Jelissa is the C.O.O. and co-founder of T & J Publications Presents, a publishing house that targets African-American men and women writers who focus on urban novels, Christian fiction, contemporary romance with a taste of street literature. Prior to co-founding her publishing company alongside her husband, Jelissa had been writing professionally since 2016.

She is a graduate of the University of Wisconsin-Madison's Odyssey Project, a course in the humanities for students facing economic barriers to college. There, she dedicated nine months to studying the works of Socrates, Plato, Dr. Martin Luther King, Jr., and many other prolific writers. She is currently pursuing an associate's degree in business management.

Jelissa has a robust publication history. On her own, she has written five books, including the following: If Loving Him Is Wrong, I Don't Want to Be Right (Parts 1 and 2) and Love Me Even When It Hurts (Parts 1, 2 and 3). Her journey as an entrepreneur and writer has been featured in both the August issue of BRAVA Magazine and in the Wisconsin CapTimes.

At the age of twenty-nine, Jelissa currently resides in the state of Wisconsin with her husband of six years and their two sons.

ALSO BY JELISSA SHANTE

If Loving Him Is Wrong, I Don't Wanna Be Right 1 & 2
Love Me Even When It Hurts 1-3

www.ingramcontent.com/pod-product-compliance
Lightning Source LLC
Chambersburg PA
CBHW061459040426
42450CB00008B/1417